THE POWER OF GOLF

THE GAME'S POSITIVE IMPACT ON THE LIVES OF THE DISABLED

U.S. ADAPTIVE GOLF ALLIANCE

THE POWER OF **GOLF**

Cover Design & Layout by Juan Pablo Ruiz
Printed in the United States of America

ISBN: 978-1-952779-08-4
Library of Congress Number: 2020923223

DEDICATED TO ALL
THE DISABLED THAT
HAVE FOUND JOY AND A
SENSE OF FREEDOM IN
THE GAME GOLF

TABLE OF CONTENTS

ACKNOWLEDGEMENTS

We are very grateful and wish to thank all those below who have taken personal time to share their stories with us so we may share these heartwarming stories with you.

Each individual, as you will learn, has overcome personal major setbacks and taken on the challenge of Golf.

In their undertaking, they've never said why me, nor said I can't.

The "POWER OF GOLF" brought them back through their own perseverance and self-dedication.

Courageous!

USAGA " Power of Golf" Players and disabilities

Tracy Ramin: Below the knee left leg amputee

Billy Fryar: wheelchair bound

Blake Harmet: Spina Bifida

Brad Schubert: Osteomyelitis, right leg amputee

Chris Biggins: Cerebral palsy. Weakened right leg

Dan Aldrich: Brachial Plexus

Darin Strenzel: Left leg amputee

John Bell: Left leg amputee

Gianna Rojas: Born with no fingers on her left hand, and left arm is underdeveloped.

Greg Hooper: Loss of vision

Jeremy Bittner: Left leg below the knee amputee

Jimmy Condon: Right leg at the knee amputee

Kim Moore: Born without a right foot, as well as a severely clubbed left foot

Steve Husome: Right leg below the knee amputee

Patti Valero: Right leg below the knee amputee

Randy Clay: Right leg at the knee amputee

Steve Shipuleski: Born with nerve damage to left hand, left leg is also shorter than the right

Steven Ford: Brachial Plexus

Kevin Holland: Cerebral Palsy, limited mobility in right arm.

Jonathan Snyder: Below the elbow limb deficiency

Brandon Canesi: Born withouth hands

PREFACE

By Phoebe S. Kaylor

"A hero is an ordinary individual who finds strength to persevere and endure in spite of overwhelming obstacles."

- Christopher Reeve

My hero is my dad, EQ Sylvester, an ordinary man who, at the age of 72, lost his two feet, his left hand, and most of his fingers on his right hand to sepsis caused by an infected kidney stone. That stone may have succeeded in taking down the average Goliath, but not my father. He not only learned to walk again but now rises each day with a greater purpose than ever before.

Through his founding of the Freedom Golf Association and the U.S. Adaptive Golf Alliance, which has 35 member organizations, his mission is to encourage the inclusion of the disabled into the fabric of society through golf. Every day he aspires to get the mentally and physically disabled onto the golf course, finding some relief and happiness while swinging a club.

My dad's story is just one heroic tale of many in this book. EQ has never wanted the focus to be on him, but rather on what he is trying to achieve in helping others. As such, this book is not about him but is a collection of stories from other heroes, each unique but with consistent themes: getting up, finding a way to succeed despite life's obstacles, and experiencing enjoyment while on a golf course.

Inspiration comes from a myriad of likely and unlikely sources. I hope that reading these true stories of individual strength and courage will become one such source of encouragement and motivation to move forward with whatever you may be looking to achieve.

"You have power over your mind--not outside events. Realize this, and you will find strength." - Marcus Aurelius

EQ not only hopes this book inspires but also invites you to join in his passion for inclusion. He believes everyone should be included in the game of golf and respective competitions but specifically strives to make adaptive golf available wherever possible. It has been said that "together we learn better." It is EQ's belief that inclusive golf not only benefits players with disabilities but creates an environment in which every player has the opportunity to flourish, thus being included in society.

Ultimately, EQ's dream is for the Paralympic Games to one day include golf, the preeminent pot at the end of his inclusion rainbow.

This is my hero's dream…what is yours?

To my hero, and to you and your aspirations, I quote Nelson Mandela:

"It always seems impossible until it's done."

-Phoebe S. Kaylor

Adaptive Golf Supporter

INTRODUCTION

What comes to mind when you think of the word "golf?" Wealthy business people at exclusive country clubs playing leisurely rounds as they hammer out business deals?

Today, the face of golf is changing. It's becoming more inclusive, in large part due to the rise of adaptive golf nationwide. I'm proud to be a supporter and promoter of this movement, and as director of the United States Adaptive Golf Alliance (USAGA) and founder of the nonprofit organization, the Freedom Golf Association (FGA). Launching this book is part of my effort to promote inclusion in the sport. Everyone's experience and journey to adaptive golf is different, but what we all share is a love of the game and the desire to see adaptive golf across all competition platforms, including the Paralympic Games. The stories in this book show why and how we can achieve this goal!

My journey to adaptive golf, creating Freedom Golf Association, and, ultimately, the United States Adaptive Golf Alliance (USAGA), begins like the stories of many other adaptive golfers. I was planning a wonderful retirement from a successful career with Fortune 500 companies and had many plans for the future when a kidney infection landed me in the hospital. The infection led to sepsis and a triple amputation.

Like so many amputees, I had to learn to live a new normal. I could swim but getting out of the pool without fingers was too difficult. Golfing was a possibility for me, but I found it difficult to find a course that could accommodate me or help me learn to play adaptive golf. Then, I did some research and found out that 20 million physically disabled people had a desire to learn to play golf but didn't do so because of their constraints and lack of access to instruction and specialized equipment. Then I knew I had a mission.

Five months after release from the hospital, I founded Freedom Golf Association, a 501(C)(3) charitable organization dedicated to bringing joy and a sense of freedom to the special needs community through their inclusion in the game of golf. We held our first clinic for adaptive golf instruction in 2013. I fondly remember one of the first students, a boy named Abraham, who was afflicted with multiple sclerosis and in a wheelchair. I remember the joy on his face when he learned how to hit a golf ball. His caretaker told me it was one of the happiest days of his life because he was normally confined to the couch most of the day. In our first year in operation, we hosted 178 adaptive golf lessons within our participation clinics.

By 2018, FGA was providing more than 6,000 adaptive golf lessons annually and reached its goal of 9,000 by the end of 2019. Our efforts have ushered more than 100 special needs golfers out onto Chicagoland golf courses, and we assisted 40 of those courses is becoming more accessible for special needs golfers. We now have about 57 individuals trained as FGA Adaptive Golf coaches, and $.74 of every $1 received goes to our special needs golf programs and events. Every year, we successfully host special clinics and competitions for all ages, including a special event with Wounded Warriors.

But the mission to have adaptive golf accepted throughout the professional golf world and on a worldwide stage cannot be achieved by FGA alone. That's why in 2015, a group of avid, world-class golfers with disabilities stepped forward and formed an important alliance called the United States Adaptive Golf Alliance (USAGA). This umbrella organization is currently comprised of 38 adaptive golf member organizations, providing nearly 40,000 disabled individuals with the joy of golf, and approximately 26 percent being combat-wounded veterans.

By making adaptive golf accessible to everyone, our member organizations address the emotional, therapeutic, and rehabilitative needs of the physically disabled, developmentally challenged, and sensory impaired, including our combat, wounded veterans. Adaptive golf gets disabled people out of bed or off the couch and introduces them to a new game or returns them to the game they once loved. USAGA uses its competitive pathway, TEACH -> PLAY -> COMPETE, to host adaptive golf instruction workshops and enhancement programs at accessible golf locations, learning centers, and international competitions.

We set out to bring disabled golf to the national stage and have succeeded through our national movement—WE SUPPORT PARA-GOLF. USAGA's INTERNATIONAL PARA-GOLF COMPETITIONS, hosted by the USAGA, promote worldwide inclusion and follow USAGA published

USAGR (U.S. Adaptive Golf Rankings) and competition standards. More than 22 national adaptive golf competitions are held by USAGA members annually across the country.

The amazing skill and talent of our world champions would be impressive if they had all their limbs, but being disabled, they're nothing short of phenomenal! Take Chad Pfeifer, who was our champion a few years ago at our competition at Pumpkin Ridge Golf Club in Oregon. He beat out the other 76 players from 10 countries who participated in the three-day tournament. He played from the blue tees, roughly 6,800 yards. Chad was a wounded warrior who lost his leg in Iraq to an IED but still shot 5 under 211. The golfer who came in second, Chris Biggins, who has cerebral palsy, came in a stroke behind. The third-place golfer was Juan Postigo from Spain, who can stripe the ball 280 yards while playing on one leg.

Talk about inspiring! And having the privilege of being in their midst, I have personally learned a great deal from my fellow disabled golfers since I took on this new mission in life. I have learned that true athletes never give up, no matter what their disability, handicap, or set back. I have learned to never ask, "Why me?" I have learned from these wonderful athletes to never say, "I CAN'T" but rather to say "I CAN." I've learned that by moving forward, we can all reach new heights in life. And, finally, I have learned that if you always reach for the high notes, your life will become very pleasurable and meaningful…I can guarantee it!

Adaptive golf is all about focusing less on what we can't do and more on what we can. Let's get para-golf included and accepted everywhere it needs to be. I invite you to join this mission of inclusion as well, so in the 2024 Paralympic Games, our para-golfers can go for the gold, just like disabled athletes can in so many other sports.

"PER ASPERA—AD ASTRA"

-Edmund Q. Sylvester

FINDING WHAT CLICKS

BILLY FRYAR

"Just like life, golf is very challenging."

I played golf my whole life, but I had to change everything after August 23, 2000. I was in a car accident where I overturned the vehicle. I broke both shoulders and seven ribs, crushed four vertebrae, and punctured both lungs. I sustained a head injury and was left in a coma for about a month. I was left paralyzed from the waist down and truly never thought I would get to play golf again.

I didn't play golf for two years after my injury because I knew nothing about adaptive golf. The Arkansas State Golf Association was located near me at the time, so I did a little research on them and figured it was time to get back into the sport I loved.

A NEW KIND OF GOLFER

I am an entirely self-taught, disabled golfer. I have spent the last several years taking what I have learned and putting it to the test at many adaptive golf tournaments around the country. Now, I am lucky to hold the number one world ranking for seated golfers. I also do some instructing for other seated golfers when I can to try and share my knowledge and encourage more seated golfers to become involved in this great game.

Eventually, I found an adaptive group to play with, and it opened up a whole new network of people who could help me learn how to play. I could also play a round with them and hang out afterward. It made all the difference in the world for me.

I have also been fortunate enough to work with people through the Arkansas State Golf Association, which has been very cool and helpful for me and seated golf in general.

Being able to teach golf is something that has always been very important to me. I do have a son who was five years old at the time of my accident, so I have been disabled most of his life. One of the first things I realized after my injury was that as he grew older, I would probably not be able to play golf with him. However, I then quickly decided this was not the mindset to have, for both our sakes. So, I began teaching him how to play, all the while teaching myself how to adapt and swing a club from a seated position. This was challenging for a lot of reasons, especially since I had spent so many years playing as an able-bodied person. Not only was I very happy to be able to teach my son how to play, but I realized my being in a wheelchair is very commonplace for him. He looks up to me just like he would if I could walk and play able-bodied golf. How important it was for him to see that disabled people are able to play golf just like everyone else!

A WINNER'S MINDSET

My playing mindset actually varies, depending on the type of environment I am facing. I know how to go out and play, have fun, and drink a few beers with the guys; that is always a fun way to golf or me. When you are playing just to get on the course, I think it is important to have fun and try not to get too frustrated if you aren't having your best game.

When I am competing, of course, I like to win. So, when the time comes, I know when I need to flip the switch, get down to business, and get really serious about it. In competition, it is important to keep a steady hand and a level head, so your emotions don't get the best of you. That kind of thing can really mess with your game.

Just like life, golf is very challenging. Golf is not for everyone; it is a sport that requires hard work and dedication. It is a love/hate sport, and a lot of people love to hate it. Life requires hard work and dedication too. It always helps to find what sports work for you because sometimes, things just click. For some people, it's hockey, basketball, or soccer, and there are a lot of different avenues people with disabilities can take. For me, it was golf, but I also play wheelchair basketball for the Arkansas Rollin' Razorbacks.

Of course, I love having opportunities to get more disabled people into the game of golf. Adaptive golf is still a young sport, but it is the right combination of fun and challenge, and that is what entices people to start playing. Getting more people into SoloRider golf carts like mine and hitting some shots grows the game, and golf is the type of sport that just works better when you have more players to compete. This is really the main reason golf is my #1 sport.

This year it was very cool to see seven seated golfers playing in the Midwest Amputee Golf Association's All Disability Open, which is the largest field of seated golfers of any other tournament so far. I would like to see the game expand and see even more seated golfers out there next year.

Billy Fryar currently lives in Bigelow, Arkansas, with his wife, Gena. His son, Dillon, is a successful car salesman, and Gena has her own health and wellness podcast. Billy is self-employed and a sales assistant to the local representative for TI Wheelchairs, the brand of wheelchair that Billy uses and absolutely loves.

Billy and his wife have a Facebook page called "It's Wheel Life." They use the page to showcase their adventures together and show that life is not that much different living with someone in a wheelchair. Gena is also interested in adaptive golf and loves traveling to watch Billy play. He says having someone with you to keep you going, who shares your passion, makes all the hard work worth it.

A LIFE OF GOLF

BLAKE HARMET

"Golf is a game that can make someone in a wheelchair, like me, feel limitless."

I like to think of golf as a game of moments. Making an ace on a tough par 3 is a great moment, but then you could have a bad moment when you double-bogey the very next hole.

My favorite golf moment was the very first time I played the game with my dad. It was right after a handicap golf cart was donated to my family's golf club. When we got down towards the green on the first hole, he looked at me and said, "Hey, we're playing golf together." For the longest time, I thought moments like that would never be possible for me.

FAMILY TRADITION

I was born with a disability called Spina Bifida and have used a wheelchair to get around my entire life. I was introduced to golf from the adaptive sports program I was in when I was a little kid. They took a group of us to the Encompass Championship and PGA Tour Champions event in Northern

Illinois. It was there that I met EQ Sylvester.

I had heard of EQ from my dad because EQ belonged to our golf club and had just started the Freedom Golf Association. During that time, I was in the middle of what would eventually be a 13-year wheelchair basketball career with the Western DuPage Special Recreation Association. I also played one year at the University of Wisconsin-Whitewater. But even with my involvement with basketball, golf was always there.

Golf has always been a huge part of my family. My dad plays golf almost every week, and my grandpa also played. My uncle not only plays golf but spent most of his career working in the golf industry for companies like Wilson, Cobra, and Titleist.

When I was about thirteen years old, I had free use of the adaptive cart at our club, so I started playing golf regularly. The cart has one seat that swivels 360 degrees, so I can swing regularly without hitting my club against the cart. At first, it was a way to get out with my dad. Eventually, I started playing with him and some of his friends. I really enjoyed showing them how the cart worked because, at the time, not many people had ever seen an adaptive cart.

At the same time, I was going to weekly golf clinics with Freedom Golf Association. I really enjoyed this because it helped me learn how to play better, and I had the chance to meet other adaptive golfers and see them play. I started to get really serious about golf at the age of 17.

FUN WITH FGA

FGA started doing annual outings, which were a lot of fun because each group had at least one adaptive golfer in their foursome. These are still played annually at Cog Hill Golf Club in Lemont, Illinois. People came from different countries to be a part of the outing. I even met people that had a family member with cerebral palsy who had come down from Canada for the event. I started playing in the outing every year and met a lot of new friends. I even played with other people from our club that I hadn't played with before.

Over the past three years, I have concentrated on practicing my golf game. I am at the practice range three or four times a week, working on my tee shots, chipping, fairway woods, and putting. Two years ago, I met Jonathan Snyder, who had just started working with FGA. As another golfer that swings one-handed, I figured he could be a good mentor, especially because he is such a solid player. Jonathan and I started doing weekly one-on-one lessons, and it did not take long before I started to see significant improvement in all areas of my game. Even when I wasn't practicing with Jonathan, I still applied what I learned in my own practice sessions. Without him, though, I would still be struggling more than I currently do.

I took Jonathan out on our course with my dad and another one of our good playing buddies, who we thought would be of equal skill, about a 7 handicap. My dad actually made a bet that Jonathan could beat the other guy while playing with one arm. Jonathan ended up losing, but it was still so cool to watch my dad and our friend react to how well Jonathan could play.

In the summer of 2020, Jonathan convinced me that I was ready to compete. I registered to play in the 2020 Midwest Amputee Golf Association's All Disability Open in Tinley Park, Illinois. Conditions at the tournament were awful, thanks to a few inches of rain that fell that week leading up to the competition date. We were even delayed a couple of hours on that Saturday. The soppy conditions were responsible for my cart dying on the 12th hole on the first day and the 13th hole on the second day. Nonetheless, participating in my first and only tournament was an incredibly cool experience. I met some wonderful people who were also very skilled golfers. Watching people with all different disabilities play golf so well was a very special time.

IN SERVICE TO GOLF

Ever since I started doing sports broadcasting in college in 2015, I knew I wanted to work in sports. I was a broadcast, print, and web journalism major. Sports broadcasting was, of course, the dream job, but it is a very hard field to get into. Sports, in general, is a very niche market.

A year after I graduated from college, I started an internship with the Chicago District Golf Association (CDGA) in April of 2019. I had a lot of different duties with the CDGA. I participated in the P.J. Boatwright Internship Program, sponsored by the United States Golf Association (USGA). While this program typically revolves around learning course marking, scoring, etc., my role was mainly with the CDGA Foundation. The CDGA Foundation has three different areas of service. They had a wounded veteran's program, a special needs program, and they are part of the nationwide Youth on Course program.

Because I use a wheelchair, I never actually thought much about working in golf, but this internship made me realize how passionate I truly am about the sport. I helped plan several different outings that also required some on-course work as well. I also worked at a number of CDGA Scramble Championship events as a foundation representative to spread the news of all the good things the foundation does.

The highlight, though, had to be getting the opportunity to go to the USGA headquarters in New Jersey. There we spent three days learning everything there is to know about working in golf. I was among 75 other interns from Allied Golf Associations all over the country. This eventually led to my participation in the making of a commercial for the U.S. Open Tournament.

I truly do not know what my life would be like right now if I didn't have golf. Golf has given me some amazing friends, life lessons, and opportunities to grow my professional career. Golf is a game that can make someone in a wheelchair, like me, feel limitless. When I am out on the course, I completely forget about my disability. It is just me, my clubs, and the course. Sure, golf comes with challenges, but I never let that bother me on the golf course. I have gone through enough hardships in my life.

Golf is how I escape all of that.

Blake Harmet is a recent college graduate who resides in Clarendon Hills, Illinois, with his parents. He has a twin sister who lives in Fort Worth, Texas, who is the only member of the immediate family who is not a golf enthusiast. However, Blake and his dad recently found her a set of clubs, so she is now learning how to play. Blake participates in FGA as a player and an ambassador, who is always trying to get people involved. He also does some part-time communications work for the United States Adaptive Golf Alliance.

THE ANTICIPATION OF GOLF

BRADLEY SCHUBERT

Over the last five years, I'd like to think that I have accomplished a great deal in the amputee community through my personality and general love for helping people rather than how well I play golf. My life-changing amputation took place in September of 2014. I lost my leg to osteomyelitis, a bone disease that causes complications for diabetics like myself. For more than eight years, I battled this illness, and after nine surgeries, which is enough for anyone in a lifetime, I decided to have my right leg amputated. Most individuals become an amputee due to a traumatic accident; it is difficult for anyone to make a conscious decision to remove part of their body. In the end, I made this choice for myself and my family, along with the full support of my wife, Heidi. My life changed not from the actual surgery on September 25, 2014, but the event I attended three weeks prior to the amputation. I have never been the same since!

INTRO TO ADAPTIVE GOLF

Two months leading up to my amputation, I started reaching out for information and support for individuals living with limb loss. I was told about an adaptive golf tournament event by some of the doctors I had been seeing leading up to my amputation. I was told it would be good for me to get involved in some support groups priors to the surgery. The golf tournament was hosted by the Midwestern Amputee Golf Association (MWAGA).

I was welcomed with open arms by then MWAGA president Jeff Linton, John Benway, and Don and Donna Zommer. These people would become family and mentors for me in my leadership in adaptive golf. After spending the day watching them play, I left the Pheasant Run Golf Resort in St. Charles, Illinois, with a sense of relief. I knew that after everything I was about to go through, I would still be able to enjoy golf and find others to support me. I told everyone I would be back to play in the event in 2015.

In the months after my amputation, I was back swinging a golf club by February of 2015. Taking the time to recover over the winter allowed me to get comfortable with my new golf swing. None of it would have been possible without the support of my family. Heidi sacrificed a lot that winter, and my daughter Brooke, who was still very young at the time, was a great nurse.

At first, I had no plans or thoughts about being a leader in adaptive golf. Then in 2016, I was asked to join MWAGA's board and was elected vice president. A year later, I became the president of MWAGA, a role I am still in today. I have hosted a number of tournaments since then, and in 2020 the MWAGA's All-Disability Open held the largest number of seated golfers in any previous USAGA sponsored event.

THE FUTURE OF GOLF

I enjoy that adaptive golf is growing here in the midwestern part of the U.S. In 2018, I was asked to become the trustee for the National Amputee Golf Association (NAGA). This was a huge honor to me because it gave me an opportunity to expose adaptive golf to more amputees all over the country.

Also, ever since meeting my MWAGA family that Sunday before my amputation, I have felt like I can help talk to others about my journey and how golf became such an important part of my life. So, I became a peer counselor for the Amputee Coalition of America, helping new amputees adjust to their new lives. I had to overcome a lot and was very grateful to help other amputees do the same. I have also become a Freedom Golf Association adaptive coach to help others use the game of golf as a form of therapy, just as I have.

I truly look forward to where my life takes me as it applies to adaptive golf, and I will end this with a final thought. You are in control of your mindset and expectations. You have to believe and work towards anything before you can achieve it. In other words, whether you think you can or you can't, you're probably right. My ultimate vision for adaptive golf is inclusion. Golf is a game that everyone can play, not just able-bodied people and not just amputees that can play on a prosthetic leg. I want to get everyone with all different disabilities into playing this game.

Brad is a multimedia designer for Cambium Networks in Rolling Meadows, IL. He creates video and e-learning content for training and education purposes. He is a father of 2 kids, Brooke, 15, and Tyler, 10. He has been married to his wife Heidi for 18 years, and he lives in McHenry, Illinois.

IT PAYS TO PUSH YOURSELF

CHRIS BIGGINS

"Getting out of your comfort zone and pushing yourself to work hard will always pay off."

I was born with a disability called cerebral palsy. This disability affects both my back and my legs. I have frequent back spasms, and my legs slightly bend when I walk. My right leg is much weaker than my left. I am able to walk, but my mobility is still significantly limited. However, even with my challenges, I'm able to enjoy the game of golf.

I have played golf almost my entire life growing up in Clarksville, Maryland. My dad worked for the local parks and recreation department, and he had a lot of friends who worked at some of our local golf courses. Often in the summer, he would take us around to play at different courses throughout the season. It was our most prevalent activity growing up, and I quickly fell in love with it. I never even thought that my disability affected my game; I just went out there and played. I took a few lessons but mainly took the time to practice on my own, and I eventually figured it out.

GOLF PRO RISING

I have always tried to be as active as I could. In addition to golf, I also played a lot of baseball as a kid. When I was a freshman in high school, I broke my foot, and I had to have foot surgery that impeded my ability to run long distances. So, I decided to completely shift my focus to golf.

When I was a sophomore, I tried out for the golf team and made it. I became very competitive, very quickly. My high school's entire team was very good, and I was actually ranked number one golfer in the county my junior year. My senior year, we won our conference championship.

It was between my junior and senior year that I realized I could really make something out of my golf game. I was eventually admitted into the professional golf management program at Methodist University in Fayetteville, North Carolina. It was while I was going to school at Methodist that I discovered all the possibilities of making a career out of golf. I did two summer internships at Woodmont Country Club in Maryland, which was near my home. At Methodist, we were always doing some sort of hands-on golf work. This included marking courses, green keeping, and learning proper instruction.

I became involved with adaptive golf at Mountainbrook Golf Club, also in Maryland. It was here that EQ was giving a speech at a fundraising event. After hearing him talk about how many people were involved in adaptive golf and how much joy people received from it, I knew right then and there that it was something that I had to join. That year, I played in my first USAGA event at Pumpkin Ridge Golf Club in Portland, Oregon.

I was very excited to be a part of tournaments that included some of the top adaptive golfers in the world. I wanted to be like them. I also wanted to be (and still do) the best adaptive golfer in the world. I came in second place, and my opponent and I were tied going into the 18th hole. On 18, he made a 30-foot putt for par. I, unfortunately, missed a two-foot putt for par, but, regardless, it was the most fun golf experience I have ever had, and it still is to this day.

A couple of years ago, I started playing in more USAGA and EDGA (European Disabled Golf Association) tournaments. I went to Dubai for the Dubai invitational, Canada, and Scotland for the Scottish Open. This tournament was especially cool because there was a European Tour going on at the same time on the same course, the Renaissance Club. We were given all the same treatment as the pros.

We participated in press conferences, had access to the player's lounge and locker rooms, and I even practiced on the driving range next to Ian Poulter and Rory McIlroy. On the last day of the tournament, my group came up to the 18th fairway, where they had a grandstand set up for the European Tour event. This, along with the whole experience of the Scottish Open, made all of us feel like we were just like the professionals.

PUSHING LIMITS

If someone with a disability similar to mine was apprehensive about getting into golf, I would challenge them by expressing how important it is as a disabled individual to push your limits. I believe in the classic saying, "The only disability in life is a bad attitude." There is a lot of truth to it. If you let yourself think you can't achieve something, then you won't achieve anything. You have to give yourself a better quality of life than that.

For me, pushing myself to become a good golfer was the best decision I have ever made. I looked at my life and said to myself, "I can really do something with this," even though, like a lot of other people with disabilities, it has not been easy for me. In fact, life itself has not been easy for me. In the end, though, getting out of your comfort zone and pushing yourself to work hard will always pay off.

Without golf, I would not have anywhere near the quality of life that I have now. I would not have made some of the best memories of my life if it weren't for golf. I have also met some of my best friends at the many golf events I have attended.

Golf is the sport that has given me the opportunity to be like everyone else. There are no pictures on the scorecard, so I have the ability to work hard and improve just like everyone else. It has given me a great quality of life. It has given me a platform to compete on a world stage, and it has given me a chance to show that I am so much more than my disability.

Chris Biggins is from Clarksville, Maryland, but currently resides in Birmingham, Alabama, eight months out of the year. The other four months, he lives in Utah, where he also trains with the U.S. Paralympic Ski Training Team as an adaptive ski racer.

In Birmingham, Chris also does a lot of volunteering with United Ability, a nonprofit organization that helps people with disabilities find work.

FINDING THE ARM GUYS

DAN ALDRICH

"The best way to recover is off the couch."

Athletics has always been a huge part of who I am. Back in high school, I played multiple sports. Golf was always a favorite, and I was one of the top players in the school with plans to play in college. However, I excelled on an international level with water ski racing.

In 1986, as a senior in high school, I was in the middle of a water ski race on the Colorado River near Lake Havasu going 100 mph when it happened. I crashed into the water, ripping out the five major nerves of my left arm (known as brachial plexus), which resulted in complete paralysis of my left arm.

I have to say that I recovered from my loss faster than most people do because I did not have any ancillary damage (like broken bones, concussion, etc.)-- just the paralyzed arm. In fact, I was released from the hospital and slept in my own bed the night I had the accident because there was nothing they could do for me immediately.

When I looked in the mirror, I didn't see a one-armed kid. I saw an athlete who happened to have only one functional arm. It was senior year, I was graduating in a week, and I had my senior trip to Hawaii coming up. There was no way I was missing it. For some reason, my brain just told me, this is your life now. Let's go!

My friend and I headed to Hawaii and one day found ourselves on the amazingly breathtaking Mauna Kea golf course. I mainly putted and chipped a few balls, but it opened a door for me. I thought maybe I could do this.

When I returned home, I went golfing with my dad, and with my first real swing as a one-armed golfer, I hammered a 4-wood right down the middle. I looked at my Dad, with joy in both of our eyes. "I CAN DO THIS!" I exclaimed.

LEARNING TO BE ONE-ARMED

Just a short few months later, I was on campus at San Diego State, planning to major in finance. I remember my biggest struggle to be carrying my tray of food from the serving counter to the table in the dining hall. Being a big eater, I grumbled about it three times a day.

Then one day, I caught sight of a fellow student in a wheelchair. He lived in the dorms and took a full load of classes, just like me. He was doing life, just like me. I watched him roll up to the table and have a cafeteria worker Velcro a fork in his hand so he could eat his meal. At that moment, the last vestige of my self-pity left me. I gratefully accepted my condition in life.

In my freshman year, I was scheduled for major surgery in Toronto, Ontario, which was where the specialist was located. It was tough to miss a few weeks, but I was back in class within six days. The surgery succeeded in rerouting two of my chest nerves to my bicep. I can now bend my elbow enough to hold up a wallet or a jacket, but that is the extent of usefulness I have with that arm.

Still, the athlete in me was healthy and strong. I worked hard on my golf game during college and learned how to snow ski with my one arm. I enjoyed ski trips throughout Canada, Whistler, Banff, Utah, and Colorado, skiing most of the hardest slopes. I still water skied but didn't race.

I learned, too, that to perform my best in any sport, I needed to get my arm out of the way. I looked for a suitable sling that would secure my arm during jostling and movement but couldn't find one. So, I fashioned a special sling of my own design that worked perfectly. I could ski, golf, and run much easier.

Years later, I was reading through a chat forum on the United Brachial Plexus Network Website (ubpn.org) and noticed that I wasn't the only one who needed to secure their arms during athletic activity. One triathlete named Robin was reaching out to find out what other people did for running. Other people replied to her, offering solutions, but none of them were as effective as the sling I had designed.

I began to work with a local supplier who helped me produce the special harness I used for water skiing. I came to them with a solid business plan for a multi-sport athletic sling, and we released our first model for customer testing in 2008. I reached out to Robin to do the honors and created a custom sling for her based on her measurements. She loved it and went on to wear the sling to many national triathlon championships. Today, the athletic sling is available on the ubpn.org website, and I have manufactured and distributed more than 1,500 throughout the U.S. and in 75 countries worldwide. It is not a money-making venture for me; profits are reinvested to help more disabled people engage in our shared love of athletic competition!

FINDING THE ARM GUYS

It was only six months after my accident when I learned of an open competition with the National Amputee Golf Association (NAGA). Since my nerves were "amputated" from my spinal cord, and I only played golf with one arm, I thought I would qualify to play. However, when I inquired, I was denied access to the tournament since I had all my digits! Ok, I thought. *I'll just keep playing golf with everyone else and competing in "normal" tournaments.* So, I did.

Fast forward to my fortieth birthday when a friend and I decided to train for a triathlon. At that event, I was introduced to the Challenged Athletes Foundation (CAF). I remember walking up to them and saying, "I'm one of you, and I've got a ton of experience. How can I help?" I did several athletic competitions with them, including more triathlons and some long-distance bicycling events.

A few years later, I was introduced to a local one-arm-golfer in Los Angeles who was the president of the Society of One-Armed Golfers, a very old and established organization based in the United Kingdom. They were having their 2012 tournament at St. Andrews in Scotland, and he invited me to attend. How could I refuse?

At that tournament, I met many more one-armed guys from the U.S. and learned of the North American One-Armed Golfer Association (NAOAGA). I was invited to their upcoming 2013 Championship game in Florida. My plan was to attend this one event but not actually get involved with the group. I had just started a business; my two children were very young, and I didn't think I had time to contribute. But I left the competition as a board member in the organization!

In late 2013, I was asked to take part in a para-long drive tournament in Mesquite, Nevada. But a week later, I received a call saying I couldn't participate because it was an amputee event, and I wasn't an amputee. Déjà vu! I had heard this line 27 years ago, but now I was older, wiser, and determined to be heard. I strongly felt that not only one-armed golfers who were not amputees, but all different disabilities should be competing together in the tournament!

I placed a call to the organizer of the event, a fellow named Dean Jarvis, to explain my position and tell him I didn't swing any differently than the one-armed golfers. I also told him I was planning to come to the event.

When Dean met me in person, he looked at me and said, "You're just an arm guy."

At that Mesquite competition, I had been the first non-amputee to play with the amputees. In the following year, that same competition had a few dozen non-amputees on the long-drive grid. Something else happened at that event too. With the inclusion of non-amputees into the tournament, the landscape of disabled golf in the United States was changed.

A collective group of us got together and conceived the umbrella organization, the U.S. Adaptive Golf Alliance (USAGA). EQ Sylvester stepped up to lead the charge and get it off the ground.

In March of 2015, I competed in the National Amputee Golf Association (NAGA) National Championship in the newly formed division for non-amputees. I had a big smile on my face and a feeling of satisfaction that it had taken a while, but I was now playing with the group that had denied me entrance so many years ago.

BECAUSE

All serious athletes, myself included, see being an athlete as part of their identity. I don't often ask the "why" of my injury because, over time, I think I've discovered some answers.

Why was I born the type of person who wouldn't let an injury keep me out of competition? Because my ability to "get over" my injury quickly helped me become an inspiration to others and show some that the best way to recover is off the couch. For decades, I have spoken to scores of audiences, including high schoolers, about my experience, my survival, the role of sports in my life, and why you should never give up.

And why am I a disabled athlete in the first place? Because I was meant to help others in special ways. I've created the athletic sling that has helped so many, and I've helped support the inclusion of the disabled in golf and the adaptive golf movement, which continues to affect thousands. My mission now is to help disabled athletes find inclusion in the activities that are so important to them, especially on the golf course.

I'm so grateful for the USAGA and all it does. Grateful not only because I personally get to compete in the events of the alliance members, but because I get to be part of the movement that ensures nobody will ever be denied, as I was so many years ago, the opportunity to participate in any competition they choose.

Dan Aldrich is the founder of Aldrich Wealth Management Group in Los Angeles and an accomplished professional and motivational speaker. He currently serves on the board of directors for the United Brachial Plexus Network and is president of the North American One-Armed Golfer Association. He competes with the Challenged Athletes Foundation (CAF). He was the founding chairperson for the Jr. Executive Board of Directors for the Make-A-Wish Foundation Los Angeles and an active Rotarian from 1994-2009. Dan is married with two children.

ADAPTING TO YOUR OWN ABILITY

DARIN STRENZEL

"See what works for you, and you will start to see positive results."

I played golf when I was a kid and really enjoyed it. I was actually pretty good too. I am tall, fast, and strong, so I was interested in other sports like basketball and baseball (with two legs), which was my main sport at the time.

NEW NORMAL

My athletic life changed in December of 2006 when an angry ex-boyfriend broke into a house where I was at a gathering with some friends. He began shooting. I was shot twice in the leg through the door. By the time it was over, two of my friends and the shooter had lost their lives. I was rushed to the hospital, and when I woke up the next day, my leg had been amputated from my hip.

After I lost my leg, I couldn't run very well anymore. As a kid, I always loved playing and competing in sports, and I couldn't stand the fact that the athletic part of my life might be over. Naturally, I started gravitating towards sports with little to no running. For a while, it was bowling, then softball, and eventually, I mustered up the strength and courage to play golf, which is an incredibly challenging sport for anyone, including able-bodied people.

Getting out on the course for the first time as an amputee was pretty exhilarating. Now, it is a huge part of my life. There are few things I enjoy more than being out on a golf course. I travel to compete in some semi-local tournaments every now and then, and I have played in three tournaments in Chicago and one in the Quad Cities, but I really just play for my own enjoyment.

GOLF BUDDIES

One of my good friends, where I live, near Peoria, Illinois, is also an amputee. He and I play a lot of golf together. I was very glad to find him because where I live, it is hard to find programs for people with amputations or disabilities who like to play golf.

Everyone in my family plays golf, so most of the time, I am out playing with them. After I was shot, I went through many dark times. My family, of course, stuck with me through all of my rehab and every aspect of my recovery. Now I am so grateful that I am able to play golf with them.

To me, golf is all about enjoyment. It is hard not to enjoy just being outside on a beautiful, warm, sunny day. But there is so much you can get out of it, too; that incredibly satisfying sound of the ball bouncing perfectly off your driver or the "plunk" of the ball dropping in the cup. Those are just a couple of things that I love about golf. You hear those sounds, and you know you're improving; you know all the work you have put in is finally paying off.

FIGURING IT OUT

If someone in my situation were looking to get into golf, I would ask them if they enjoy playing. That is the most important part. If you enjoy it but still struggle with learning how to play, then you must figure out what works best for you based on your ability, whether you have an arm or leg amputation or another disability. For me, mastering my balance on my prosthetic was what really made things a lot easier for me.

I swing differently than any other player out there because we all have our own unique style that works for us. Often, this is something you might have to figure out on your own. I have worked with PGA Professionals before, and most of the time, they have a lot of trouble understanding how my body works. So, go out to the practice range, hit some balls, take tips from whoever might have some to offer, see what works for you, and you will start to see positive results.

Darin Strenzel currently lives in Morton, Illinois. He earned a Bachelor of Science degree in accounting from Bradley University and now works for Caterpillar, Inc. Darin married his high school sweetheart, Carla, and has three wonderful children and a Great Dane.

ONE SWING AT A TIME

JOHN BELL

"A challenge is always good."

On October 7, 2011, I was rear-ended by a truck while riding on a motorcycle, and life as I knew it was forever changed. The doctors and medical staff worked to save my life, and I woke up three days later after being in a medically-induced coma, with no idea about the extent of my injuries. A good friend was the one who had to tell me my left leg had been amputated. I also broke my back, several ribs, and my left arm. My left hand was completely destroyed from being launched into the headlight of the truck, and I had to have a plate put into my skull. A traumatic brain injury kept me in ICU for 30 days.

ADAPTING

Losing my leg didn't seem like it was going to be that bad. My first thoughts were that I'd get one of those cool running blades like the guys you see on TV and be on my way. I was automatically in recovery mode. I have always been a fighter and have always had the "it is what it is" attitude. It wasn't until I arrived home from the hospital and had to start adjusting to my new normal that I realize,d "wow, this sucks," and I knew life was going to be a lot harder than I thought.

Six months later, after dealing with painful neuromas and a bone spur, I had to go back in for a second amputation and go through the healing process all over again. At least recovery this time around was just my leg, but I still spent 11 months in a wheelchair before getting a prosthetic. And then the real adjustment period began; the constant discomfort and pain, constant trips to the prosthetic doctor, the realization of never going back to my job in construction.

Once I was healed enough to be able to get a prosthetic and walk again, I had a ton of time to think. Well, my bright idea was to go and pick up golf again as I knew it was very low impact and great for walking. I went to a fitter and ended up with a brand-new set of golf clubs. It was time to adapt and overcome as my golf swing was drastically different from the last time I had played.

In 2013 I met my wife, married, and moved to Florida. I was lucky enough to find a nearby driving range where I could practice. They have these machines where you can get a hopper of golf balls, and it auto loads the ball on the tee so I could work on swinging and adjusting my stance without having to bend down and adjust the ball on the tee after every swing.

In late 2017, I played a team scramble with my friend James who is also an above-the-knee amputee, and we won. It was safe to say I was hooked on adaptive golf.

LIFE IN ADAPTIVE GOLF

I have played and competed in many events and also assisted adaptive clinics over the last two years for a number of organizations around the country. I was also picked to represent the United States as the vice-captain of the USA ParaGolf Team during 2018's Ryder Cup-style format event. In the first part of 2020, I had the opportunity to travel to Celtic Manor in the United Kingdom for the captain's meetings for the upcoming Cairns Cup (postponed until 2021 due to COVID-19). Soon after arriving home, I was asked to be an adaptive team staff member for Callaway Golf.

Over the last couple of years, I have seen significant improvement in my game just from playing with other strong, adaptive golfers. Even though we are often competing against each other, we all have to adapt, so we are always trying to help each other play better.

I love competing because of the camaraderie. Everyone is very similar in their abilities, so it is very easy to bounce ideas off of people about golf and life in general. I have played in about two dozen tournaments over the last three years.

One of my other favorite parts of competing is traveling across the country and even the world and having the opportunity to play amazing courses with other adaptive athletes.

I also have my own personal brand, OneLegBell. I use the

brand and nickname as an attention-getter to gravitate people towards adaptive golf. My main reason for this is to showcase the capabilities of amputees. The brand is something another amputee can look at and say, "Hey, I can do that."

I would challenge someone in a similar situation to mine to find a purpose in life, whatever that may be. Even if trying something new might scare you, it never hurts to go out and try. I never want to see anyone struggle. If someone says, "I'll never be as good as you," I reply, "I hope you will be better than me," because a challenge is always good. Out on the course, I always tell people, "Hit it, go find it, and hit it again." Keep plugging away and enjoy it. Life has endless opportunities everywhere. Don't give up; go out and try everything, including golf.

One of the best things I have received from adaptive golf is the ability to help kids of all abilities get into the game. When you are watching a kid enjoy golf, it feels indescribably good. They say kids are the future, and since golf is mainly played by elderly people, they are truly the future of both adaptive and able-bodied golf. That is actually the reason we promote golf for absolutely everyone. It is an all-inclusive sport, and I am personally always trying to support that concept.

John Bell is married with two stepdaughters and lives in Weeki Wachee, Florida, the City of Mermaids. He also helps with the Never Say Never Foundation, The Amputee Coalition, the North American One-Armed Golfers Association and the Cairns Cup, a biannual, transatlantic event.

ONE-HANDED LADY GOLFER

GIANNA ROJAS

"Golf is my purpose, my identity."

Yes, you read that right. I was born in 1962 with no fingers on my left hand; my left arm is underdeveloped compared to my right. My mom took a pill called Thalidomide, which was given to women to help with morning sickness when she was pregnant with me. Soon afterward, doctors began noticing that it caused children to be born with missing limbs.

As a kid, I was beaten up, called names, pushed aside, and left out, feeling unwanted and alone. It's something they now call bullying. To make matters worse, my father was in the Navy, and like many military families, we moved every couple of years. I was always the new kid, and that made things much harder on me.

GOLF AS INCLUSION

I became interested in golf about 10 years ago, thanks to my husband of 35 years. He is an avid golfer with all of his friends and his friend's wives. When they would go out, they would call me when they got to the 15th hole to meet them for lunch, and I would. Sometimes they would go back out, and I would go back home alone. I began to feel left out like I did as that 13-year-old girl who was beaten up and called names. I just really wanted to spend more time with him, so I began going to the driving range, trying to find a way to learn golf.

I am mostly self-taught through trial and error. It was the fact that I was teaching myself that gave me the idea that people with disabilities need proper instruction, as do the instructors.

I was the first woman from the United States to sign up for the World Ranking for Golfers with Disabilities in January of 2019, a designation by the Royal and Ancient Golf Club (R&A) and the United States Golf Association (USGA). I don't think I am good enough to win any trophies yet. Although I do enjoy competing, I am not actually in it for the competition. I do it mainly to be visible and an example for young women and girls with disabilities that might be doubting the fact that they can get out and play golf. I hope they look at me and say, "Hey, if she can do it, I can too."

In actuality, the ball and the hole do not care if you roll it with your nose or if it evens get there. It is about the example you are setting. Plus, there are significant mental health benefits behind being outside, enjoying good company, and doing something you love.

The other draw is the camaraderie on both sides. My first exposure to international competition was in 2017, at the United

States Disabled Golfer's Association (USDGA) Open. I was incredibly impressed to see how many disabled golfers from all over the world traveled to Rotunda, Florida, to compete in that tournament. The resilience of all these adaptive golfers is truly amazing, and I am proud and honored to be a part of the community. I now have friends in Scotland and all over Europe that I never would have met if it weren't for the game of golf.

IN SERVICE TO ADAPTIVE GOLFERS

In 2017, I founded Adaptive Golfers, a non-profit 501 (c) (3) to empower individuals with different (not dis) ABILITIES to use golf as an emotional and physical therapeutic activity. We also have several strategic marketing campaigns aimed at specific groups: Adaptive GolfHERs, which targets women and young girls with disabilities, and then there is our Adaptive GolfHEROs, a campaign that targets veterans and first responders. These brands are our way to gain exposure to people of all different demographics, gender, status, age, and, most importantly, different abilities. All are welcome!

We have worked with a lot of people who have different challenges. Some have had significant mobility restrictions, including stroke survivors that have trouble walking and using their hands. They sometimes enter a deep depression that can be debilitating alongside their actual physical limitations. Golf is a fun way to break through that. We had one specific participant whose wife called me because she was worried that she was losing him because he was getting so depressed. He began attending our clinics and progressed very nicely. Now he goes out to the course regularly with his friends, even if he doesn't play much. It is all very moving.

In 2017, I asked Reed Expo, who runs the Professional Golfers' Association (PGA) Show, if they would consider adding an Adaptive Resource Center to the show's floor. Much to my surprise, they said yes! We have had a spot at both the Orlando Merchandise Show and the Las Vegas Fashion and Demo experience for the past four years. It is always cool to see how attendees react when we ask them to try and swing a club blindfolded, from a seated position, or one-armed. Their first thought is, I can't do that. Well, that is the first thought a new adaptive golfer has too. However, whether someone is disabled or able-bodied, when they try to swing like an adaptive golfer, they realize it is not hard; it is just different. What is most important is how you conquer that feeling.

I was also introduced to a young woman in South Carolina. When we first met, she was so nervous she started hugging me. She began telling me how long she had been watching me on social media and how badly she wanted to learn to play. As someone with one arm who had never seen anyone play one-armed golf before, she wasn't sure if she could. She took the same leap I did, and now she is a golfer herself.

TRIAL AND ERROR

Adaptive golf is all about inclusion and diversity. Anyone can play. Big organizations like PGA, Ladies Professional Golf

Association (LPGA), R&A, and the USGA are beginning to get that message out. Inclusion for people with disabilities in golf is gaining awareness and acceptance.

If you are apprehensive about playing golf, just get out and try it. Keep your expectations realistic, and be willing to try something new. I tell my participants not to ask themselves, "Can I," but, instead, ask, "HOW can I?" By doing so, you give yourself the opportunity for trial and error that will help you decide if you actually like it. You never know until you try, and I think there is no point in looking at something and automatically thinking, I can't do that.

For individuals with disabilities, it is more about shifting the mindset away from the question, "Can I?" It's about empowering them to take equity in their own quality of life, mind, body, and soul. We are just using golf as the conduit.

For the golf and allied health industries, you can add this other layer of instructional approaches with our formal training. Then comes the challenge of getting the right people to teach the sport on top of their own game and cater that to all abilities. I have worked closely with the LPGA, PGA, and other European organizations like the European Disabled Golfers Associations. I never asked for involvement; they just found me, and I am extremely grateful for them. If it wasn't for these allied organizations, golf would not be as inclusive as it is today. I serve as someone who can use her own experience to influence other disabled athletes to get into golf, so they can get as much out of it as I have.

Golf has become my purpose, my identity. Golf has shown me why I was born this way. I look at myself as a messenger to show people what I, along with thousands of other disabled people, are able to do. We have to be able to convey our capabilities if the adaptive golf industry is going to make a difference. As long as our heart is in the right place, good things are going to happen.

Gianna Rojas is a 58-year-old, golfin' grandma with two knee replacements, a soon-to-be-replaced hip, a bad back, and one hand. She is out on the golf course to walk the talk of what she preaches—that golf is inclusive and a game for anyone. She has been married for 35 years to a beautiful man and has two daughters, age 33 and 34. Her youngest daughter is in and out of the Marines, carrying on

the family tradition of military service. Her older daughter has two sons, three and five years old. Her youngest grandson has autism, so Gianna will work to get him the same fair treatment and inclusion that she has enjoyed. Gianna lives in Oak Ridge, New Jersey, and has a second residence in North Myrtle Beach, South Carolina. She is the CEO and Founder of Adaptive Golfers, a 501 (c)(3) nonprofit organization, bringing golf to individuals with different ABILITIES.

SEEING THE VALUE OF GOLF

GREG HOOPER

"Golf is always my happy place."

I have a connective tissue disease that affects several parts of my body. At the age of 17, I lost most of the sight in my left eye. When I was 35, I was in a car accident, which caused a tear in my right eye, so I lost sight in that eye as well. I still have decent peripheral vision, but no vision at all if I look straight ahead.

I started playing golf when I was eight years old, long before I lost my sight. It was something I loved to do as a kid, but it was mainly just a fun hobby. After I lost my eyesight in my right eye, it took over a year before I started playing again. This was tough because I had played with eyesight in both eyes, then one, and now none.

FRIENDS AND GOLF

By nature, I'm a competitive person, and that competitive drive is something I really value having in life. I've learned that the key to playing golf with no eyesight is repetition. It was quite the process to re-learn the game, but once I had my swing down, I was able to consistently make contact with the ball. I did not get there on my own; thankfully, blind golf is a team sport. It couldn't be done without a coach there with you along the way. They help place me in the direction of the fairway and help with the position and angle of the club and the line for putting.

Blind golfers must swing the club the exact same way every time, which is different from golfers with sight. The coach helps account for draw or slice on the shot as well. Playing tournament golf as a blind player is a lot more work. Everything is much more meticulous.

Because I had played the game for so long before I lost my sight, I did not find it all that difficult to pick it up again. It was just learning the particular swing that worked well for me so that I came through the ball at the same time and place, every time.

I also had to change up which clubs I would play for certain shots. This was easy because I have a lot of friends that helped me long before I started competing in 2010. They refused to let me walk away from playing just because I had lost my sight.

Almost every company I have ever worked for had some kind of golf league. So, I started playing on a weekly basis. My work colleagues and other friends that golfed with me weren't actually coaches, but they have always done a good job of helping my line up. I just figured out my swing from there. I was frustrated and lost a lot of balls, but after hitting hundreds and hundreds of balls on the range for two or three years, I started playing like my old self. If I didn't have those friends with me, I would not be playing this sport.

I became so invested in adaptive golf that I eventually became the President of the United States Blind Golfers Association (USBGA). We have a juniors' program, where we work with other organizations to recruit blind kids to play with us. Some of the kids are with the STARS (social, therapeutic, academic, and recreational services) program here in Atlanta for the Center for the Visually Impaired. In 2013 we had our first clinic with them, and we had 31 kids in attendance. We also had the USBGA championship at that same time, so the high-level blind players competing in that tournament had a chance to teach the kids.

Initiating new programs to promote blind golf has been my full-time job since leaving the workforce in 1999. We work with AVID (A Vision in Darkness) in Nashville, which is another program that works with the Tennessee School for the Blind. We have helped them do the same kind of program as STARS. We also have our veterans' program, in which we partner with the PGA Hope. We teach them the fundamentals, then work to get them a coach so they can get out onto the course.

We are constantly working to grow our numbers of players and volunteers. I don't want a kid to ever have someone tell them they can't do something just because they are visually impaired. We always start easy with them, just teaching them how to make contact with the ball. They take off from there, and we have several kids that now play regularly with their families. That is a success for us.

DIFFERENT STROKES FOR DIFFERENT FOLKS

Teaching someone with a visual impairment and teaching someone who is totally blind are two very different things. For a person who used to have sight, it easier for them to remember how to swing and where the ball should be. For a person who is totally blind, it is all about mobility training. We teach them that the club is a connection to the ground and to move the club like you are trying to make contact with the ground, not the ball. With someone who has minimal vision, you have to deal with the environment, including the ground, sunlight, trees, etc. For them, the ground acts as a visual aid. They have the sensory input of the club making contact with the ground. They know how to swing the club because they feel it hit the ground through their hands.

I challenge all people all the time. Many of the people who come to us have never picked up a club, even if there was a time when they could see. For us at the USBGA, we just challenge them to take that first step of picking up a club and seeing how it feels. We also have people who played the game when they could see and now lost their sight. We challenge them to work hard to find their balance and make contact with the ball. Once they can do that, their confidence soars, and they fall in love with the game. From then on, they become much more comfortable contacting the ball and continuously working on their swing to maintain that consistency. We also try to always teach people that golf should be fun. We don't want it to be something that frustrates or bores them.

Golf is always my happy place. The golf course is where I know I can be successful, and it helps me maintain some sense of sanity in this crazy world. Before I lost my sight, I traveled for 25 years as an engineer. During that time, it was hard to find what made me happy. Now, I have so many great friends who play golf with me, and I would not have them if it weren't for the game. Also, as a teacher of golf, it is very self-gratifying to see other blind golfers become successful on the course. As a competitor, it keeps me driven and determined to reach my goals and win championships. My competitive spirit pushed me onto the course when I was unsure of myself. Now it keeps me on the course, competing and helping other blind individuals discover the value of golf in their own lives.

Greg Hooper is currently president of the USBGA and an avid volunteer with the Georgia State Golf Association for adaptive golfers and several other organizations around Atlanta, Georgia. He has been married for more than twenty years and is the father of four grown children ages 41, 36, 34, and 22. When his children were in school, he volunteered with the high school music programs and now helps direct marching bands all over Georgia. When not volunteering or building furniture, you'll find Greg out on the course, playing golf.

THE REWARDS OF ADAPTING

JEREMY BITTNER

"If you don't challenge yourself, you will just become stuck."

In July of 1993, when I was four years old, I was following behind my dad's riding lawn mower with a plastic mower that made bubbles when I pushed it. My dad thought I had stopped trailing him, so he backed up when I wasn't looking. As a result of the accident, I lost my lower left leg below the knee. Three weeks and five surgeries later, I was discharged from the hospital. After extensive physical therapy, I was able to walk by my birthday that October. For Christmas that year, I received a pair of skis and used them in my backyard that very day. I guess you could say I was an unstoppable athlete.

AMPUTEE ATHLETE

Growing up, I played all kinds of sports, despite my amputation. In my hometown of Williamsport, Pennsylvania, Little League baseball is king. In addition to playing baseball through high school, I also played basketball, hockey, skiing, racquetball, and backyard football.

When I was 15, I fell in love with the game of golf. My dad would drop me off at the course with a friend on the way to work and pick us up at the end of the day. A few years later, I had even fewer rounds under 100, so I decided to try out for the high school golf team. I made the team as a freshman but didn't play in any tournaments. The following year I was cut from the team during tryouts.

It was at that point I realized that if I wanted to play this sport competitively, it would take more than just casually playing every once in a while. The team got a new coach who put me on the team the next year. Then, at the conclusion of the season, he contacted everyone, saying if they wanted to work with him at the simulator in the offseason, he would be available. I was the only one to reach out.

Working with him once a week, we were able to rebuild my swing into something repeatable with a focus on weight transfer. Up until that point, I had quite a bit of difficulty transferring weight onto my leading left leg. This led to a pronounced cut/slice. By widening my stance a bit, I was able to transfer my weight effectively without losing balance on my prosthetic leg. At that point, my career-best round was 83. In my first round following my winter swing rebuild, I shot 82.

From that point on, my love for the game has only increased. Shortly thereafter, the pro at my local course asked if I had ever heard of the Eastern Amputee Golf Association

(EAGA). He gave me some information, and I signed up for my first tournament, the Pennsylvania Amputee Open in Carlisle, Pennsylvania. At that tournament, I was able to meet golfers of all ages and disabilities and saw how they had adapted their swing to better their game. Leg, arm, above the knee, below the knee, double amputees…nothing stopped these guys from getting out there and competing to win their flight or the entire tournament. The camaraderie after the round was just as important as the golf itself. The hospitality suite was filled with golfers, their friends, and family. It was apparent that the tournaments served an even greater purpose to nearly everyone there. It gave them a chance to share stories with people who had similar experiences, yet everyone had their own unique story about how they came to discover adaptive golf.

STEPPING UP THE GAME

Over the years, I was able to further refine my craft and lower my handicap to scratch. This was in thanks to extensive practice and the right coaching. Overall, the time I spent on my own making improvements in my game was what really made the difference. I was also able to win several amputee tournaments, including the 2007 Pittsburgh Amputee Open, 2008 Pennsylvania Amputee Open, 2010 Buffalo Amputee Open, and 2018 EAGA Eastern Regional Championship. I have also placed in the top five at the 2018 and 2019 National Amputee Golf Association (NAGA) National Championship.

Playing in these events over the years, I was grateful to

have had an opportunity to develop friendships from across the country and learn invaluable lessons both on and off the course. Finding out you are not alone in your various struggles as an amputee is a fantastic way to work through them. Finding out different methods to ease aches and pains and sharing some of your own remedies goes a long way towards helping others and helping yourself too.

I am so grateful to organizations like EAGA, NAGA, the U.S. Disabled Golfers Association (USDGA), and the U.S. Adaptive Golf Alliance (USAGA) for bringing us together. The individuals that run these organizations are helping people who might not otherwise know where to turn. Participating in these events for the past 15 years has given me something to look forward to during every golf season and pushed me to become a better version of myself.

ADAPT AND ACHIEVE

I would challenge someone to get out and play golf because whatever your disability, there is always a way to adapt and play the game well. You are going to find things you can do like everyone else and also challenges that require you to find a different way to swing, stand, etc. Taking the effort to find how to adapt the game in a way that works for you will always pay off in the long run. If you don't challenge yourself, you will just become stuck.

Golf has been something I have always loved. It did not come naturally to me, but from the first time I stepped onto the course, I have kept coming back. Golf teaches humility, camaraderie, and if you work hard enough, you will receive sweet rewards. Golf has a way of always pushing me. It is a constant challenge that always keeps you on your toes. For me, it's also an important motivational tool. And that in itself is a sweet reward!

Jeremy Bittner lives in Pittsburgh, Pennsylvania, and works as an assistant general manager at a luxury hotel, where he impresses people with his stamina for standing on his feet all day with an amputated leg. He is engaged to a wonderful woman named Darlene, and they have a 7-year-old boy and a 3-year-old girl. Jeremy golfs as much as he can during the season and also plays wheelchair basketball in the winter. He has had a few appearances at the National Wheelchair Basketball Association's national tournament and has been selected a few times for the all-tournament team.

A PASSION FOR THE GAME

JIMMY CONDON

"The hard times in my life have taught me to stay level-headed while playing golf."

In April of 2014, I was in a motorcycle accident and lost my right leg at the knee. Before then, I never played golf. I ran a lot of races and was athletic and active, but golf never crossed my mind.

After I became injured, I needed something to stay busy. I also wanted to find an escape from all the hustle and bustle of Los Angeles, where I was living at the time. I had a couple of friends that played golf, so I figured the sport might be the perfect escape for me. It quickly became so much more. Not only did I begin to quickly see improvement in my game, but I realized I could use golf as a way to show people what amputees could do. Even though I did not play well at all when I first started, I loved the fact that I could get out and play. I also knew that even though I couldn't be the same athlete I once was, I knew that if I worked at it, I could play golf at a high level.

A VOICE FOR ADAPTIVE GOLF

It was then that I noticed more of my friends wanting to get involved. They saw my developing passion for the game, and I think some of it actually rubbed off on them. I eventually made my way down to Orlando, Florida, for my first tournament hosted by the U.S. Disabled Golf Association (USDGA) in 2017.

Once I arrived, I was blown away at how many people were participating in the event. I truly had no idea adaptive golf was so popular. The first two people I met were Jonathan Snyder and Tracy Ramin. Jonathan had just started working with Freedom Golf Association (FGA), and since I am a native of Lemont, Illinois, he convinced me to move back and get involved with FGA.

I started as a participant, just trying to improve my own game as much as I could, with the help of the FGA coaches. After a while, I started mentioning to Jonathan that I wanted to become more involved in the mission of FGA. After some more discussion with Jonathan, I was hired as the director of marketing for Freedom Golf Association.

I spent a lot of time continuing to go to clinics, but instead of playing, I spent my time speaking with participants and learning their stories to put out on our website and social media platforms. My main goal was to spread the word about FGA and our amazing, capable participants. While I only held this position for a few months, I met many incredible golfers. I also learned that there are a lot of people out there in worst situations than me who have worked very hard to learn how to play golf well. It was also during this time that our following and donors really increased dramatically as we grew in size.

After getting involved with FGA, I realized that I had a mission to promote inclusion in golf. The sport has done so much for me. Now, it is a huge part of my life. If the weather is right, I try to play once or twice a week. I also have traveled all over the Midwest, competing in adaptive golf tournaments. Most recently, I won my flight in the All Disability Open at Odyssey Golf Club in Tinley Park, Illinois. This event was hosted by the Midwest Amputee Golf Association (MWAGA). I have also competed in events with the Iowa Amputee Golf Association and the Wisconsin Amputee Golf Association. If it weren't for U.S. Adaptive Golf Alliance (USAGA) umbrella organizations like the MWAGA, I wouldn't have the opportunity to travel, compete, and meet new people with disabilities that match my enthusiasm for the game of golf. I am very thankful for that.

STRENGTH FROM EXPERIENCE

Like most players, I still have my struggles, and I still get frustrated with golf every now and then. I have my strengths, like my tee shots. My driver goes about 250 yards. It's in times of trouble with golf that I am actually thankful to have gone through all that I have. The hard times in my life have taught me to stay level-headed while playing golf. I don't get frustrated easily, and I am not bothered if I have a bad round.

I know that golf is something I will do as long as I am

able. As someone who endured such a terrible accident at such a young age and is still able to play, I feel like I am capable of playing until I'm 90 years old. While that may or may not happen, I know that my passion for golf is here to stay. Even if I do get to a point where I can no longer play, I know that won't mean that I'll stop caring about the game.

I am thankful that I have been able to watch adaptive golf grow around the country, and I know this is just the beginning. I know there are a lot of other amputees like me who love golf as well. I believe those other amputees who share my passion will continue to raise awareness and grow the game of adaptive golf. I feel very lucky to have been a part of that for many years.

Jimmy Condon is currently living in Orland Park, Illinois, and working in real estate as the manager of four rental properties. Although no longer with Freedom Golf Association as an employee, he still plays golf and volunteers with them. There is rarely a time Jimmy wishes he was not out on the golf course or a driving range, working on his game. In addition to FGA, he also stays involved with the U.S. Adaptive Golf Alliance and the Midwest Amputee Golf Association.

PASSING IT ON

KIM MOORE

"I have seen firsthand how golf changes people's lives."

Unlike a lot of amputee golfers, I actually did not sustain any life-changing injury. I was born without a right foot, as well as a severe clubbed left foot. I have a prosthetic leg that starts just below my knee. I have also undergone numerous surgeries on my clubbed foot and have a small degree of spina bifida, but that doesn't significantly affect my abilities.

I came from a pretty sports-oriented family. Growing up in Fort Wayne, Indiana, I always played basketball. In Indiana, that is definitely the most popular sport to play. I was always able to play, despite my disability, but I wasn't all that fast and sometimes struggled with my balance. Eventually, I realized I wanted to find a new sport where I was able to be a little more competitive. I thought of golf and tried out for the golf team my freshman year of high school. I made the junior varsity team, and I played in my first ever golf tournament that year. To my own surprise, especially since I played against able-bodied golfers, I actually won the tournament!

GOLF CAREER

It really took off from there. I started playing more and more in the summer and even got my first job working at a local golf course. I went on to win a couple more tournaments my junior and senior year of high school, this time with the varsity team. I became a pretty recognizable face, and I think my disability attracted a lot of attention. Nonetheless, I just put my head down and continued to practice and play the best I could. That paid off, and I eventually earned a full golf scholarship to the University of Indianapolis. I was still the only amputee around, but I went on to win about 12 tournaments for the team throughout my four years at the college. Senior year I won the Kim Moore Spirit Award, which was named after me. Now, that award goes to a division 3 athlete, a division 2 athlete, and a division 1 athlete and coach.

My junior year was when I made the decision to actually pursue golf as a career. At the time, I was studying biology and chemistry and had plans to go on and become a doctor. After college, I began competing against other amputees. I started playing locally in the Indiana Women's Amputee Tournament. I won it the first time I played and decided I wanted to keep competing. I was introduced to the National Women's Amputee Golf Tournament. I won that tournament 13 years in a row.

I was introduced to coaching at Indiana-Purdue University at Fort Wayne as an assistant. I knew I wanted to coach, but in a different environment than a club or a public course. I did spend 12 years at Colonial Oaks Golf Course in Fort Wayne. I started working there cleaning golf carts and helping with some other member services. I worked my way up to the pro shop, and I eventually became the assistant professional at the course. After that, I became a PGA pro. I eventually worked my way up to playing professionally in the Women's Futures Tour, now known as the Symetra Tour, the development tour for the Ladies Professional Golf Association. I tried for the LPGA in Qualifying school and unfortunately missed the cut by one stroke.

For the last eight years, I have been the head golf coach at St. Mary's University, the sister school to Notre Dame. I was very lucky to find this position because it is a great program, and it gave me a chance to pursue my career locally. I have always loved my home state.

At St. Mary's, I have enjoyed coaching and having the opportunity to show people that amputees are capable of playing golf at a high level. I am able to do that through coaching, and that truly means a lot to me.

As a team, we have had our fair share of struggles. However, in the last five years (2015-2020), we have found some more success and have been quite competitive in our division and conference. In the last three years, we have won our conference. In the last two years, we have gone to the NCAA Tournament. We have reached a number 13 overall national ranking.

SHARING THE GAME

I have had the chance to work with some truly incredible golfers. I have coached conference MVPs, all-conference players, all-Americans, and academic all-Americans. Today, I still have the chance to teach and instruct outside of my team at Saint Mary's. I currently work as the director of instruction at Knollwood Country Club, which is also Saint Mary's home course. I have also developed an annual clinic in my hometown of Fort Wayne, specifically for new amputee golfers. This means a lot to me because I have been very fortunate to play at a high level as an amputee, and I love helping other amputees do the same.

Golf is a game that different people with different abilities can play. Just because you have a disability doesn't mean you can't play. I have seen so many people with different abilities become very successful golfers.

One of the reasons I play is because it gives me a sense of normalcy. I have seen many people with different abilities become remarkably successful in golf. At SRT Prosthetics and Orthotics, I even helped quadriplegics learn how to swing a club. I challenge people to take lessons and get out and try golf. I can't encourage that enough. Some people can even work up the skills to compete with able-bodied golfers.

My goal has always been to promote the ability of amputee golf because I have seen firsthand how golf changes people's lives. Golf has allowed me to have so many opportunities in my life. Without golf, I would not have the career I have; I would not have traveled all over the world, and I would not have met some of my best friends. I am a coach because I want to pass on the love of the game. I want to give other people the same incredible chance to do something great in their lives, maybe even with the game of golf.

Kim Moore currently lives in South Bend, Indiana, with her 7-month-old Chocolate Lab named Scotty. Scotty is, of course, named after Scotty Cameron, of Scotty Cameron Putters. She is the youngest of three children and has an older brother and sister and many nieces and nephews. Her parents, who have always been supportive of her golfing, not only enjoy watching Kim golf but have developed an enthusiasm for other competitive disabled golfers and adaptive golf as a sport.

MY NEXT SHOT

STEVE HUSOME

"The game of golf will teach you important lessons about life."

It was a beautiful September day in Iowa when my life was forever changed in the blink of an eye because of one split-second decision. I was heading out towards Des Moines on my motorcycle with friends to see a concert, which was about a two-hour ride from Cedar Falls. About forty minutes into the ride, I came upon two semi-trucks driving extremely slow for a 55-mph roadway. As I prepared to pass them, the lead truck turned right in front of me. Without any time to react, I slammed into the driver's side of the cab and was pulled underneath the vehicle.

The first responders pulled me from the wreckage, and I was flown by helicopter to one of the best trauma hospitals in the state. The doctors raced to save my right leg. My injury was described as a "degloving" injury from my knee to my toes on the right leg. The knee on my left leg was severely dislocated. All four ligaments in the knee joint were torn away from the bone. My right elbow was shattered. The first several days at the hospital were a blur. I was in and out of the operating room every day for four days until the doctors gave me the worst news possible: "We have about a 70 percent chance we can save your right leg, but only about a ten percent chance you will ever have any function in your knee or ankle." He went on to give me the option of amputation.

For four days, I lay there and pleaded with my wife, "Don't let them take my legs." I didn't want to come out of surgery one day only to discover they had cut off my legs. Finally, after a lot of soul searching and discussion, I made the impossible decision to amputate my right leg. My medical team did a fantastic job of screwing my knee together and adding plates to the tibia and fibula to perform the amputation about six inches below the knee. As I discovered, being a below-knee amputee versus above the knee is an enormous difference.

At 54 years old, I had to be rebuilt, not only physically but mentally as well. I was faced with many months of more surgery, healing, and physical therapy just to learn how to walk again.

FINDING ANSWERS

I have always loved the game of golf. I started playing when I was 12 years old and have loved the game ever since. The game of golf will teach you important lessons about life.

One of my favorite quotes is from the great Bobby Jones, who said, "*Golf is the closest game to the game we call life. You get bad breaks from good shots; you get good breaks from bad shots – but you have to play the ball where it lies.*" I was faced with a very bad break, just as my life was going very well. I knew it was going to take courage and determination to improve my strength, endurance, and emotional well-being. But my goal was to get back onto the golf course.

Goal setting has helped me throughout my career and ultimately motivated me to get my life back. Many people say you find your "new normal," but I didn't accept that. There was no more "normal" for me. My leg wouldn't magically grow back and allow me to be normal again. So, I needed to find the right kind of motivation to rebuild myself into the new me, a better version of what I was before the accident.

I started by taking a good look at myself in the mirror. I asked myself, who am I? How do I want to be remembered? How can I be a better husband, father, grandfather, brother, and son? It was this soul searching that sprouted the idea to form a non-profit foundation to help other people who had to experience the same thing I did. When I was faced with the decision to amputate my leg, there wasn't anybody supportive to talk to about finding prosthetics or living with limb loss. I was determined to become the best resource possible for people facing amputation.

The HusomeStrong Foundation is now four years old, and we have grown the organization from our meager beginnings to a well-funded endowment to assist amputees financially. I have worked closely with the Amputee Coalition of America to become a certified peer visitor and lead advocate to address legislative initiatives that protect and assist people in the limb loss community.

BACK TO WINNING

Two years after my accident, I was able to return to the golf course to play a round of golf. This was one of the best days of my life. I was also able to play with my son, who had returned home after eight years of military service. I didn't have any expectations about my ability to swing a club or worry about my next shot. I just played the game and enjoyed the beautiful day.

I discovered that my swing certainly needed more work, but the foundation was still there. I had achieved my goal of returning to golf, but the work was just beginning.

I quickly learned there was an Iowa Amputee Golf Tournament held every year in July. I reached out to Andy Devine, a PGA professional who has helped me develop my golf swing over the past 20 years. I told Andy about my goal to enter this tournament and be competitive. The game of golf is a great vehicle for people with varying degrees of "ability" (not disability) to challenge themselves and find motivation and purpose.

After a third-place finish in my first Iowa Amputee Tournament, I was hooked. I met some wonderful people from all over the Midwest, traveling to Iowa annually to see old friends and play in this event. I also discovered there were many more tournaments to enter. I was encouraged and determined to improve my game and play in as many events as possible over the next year.

On September 12, 2017, three years to the day after my amputation, I was crowned the champion of the Midwest Amputee Golf Tournament in Chicago. I was extremely proud to share the moment with my golf mentor, Andy, who was so instrumental in instilling confidence in me to compete and play at a high level. I went on to compete in the 2018 National Amputee Golf Tournament in Michigan.

FOR THE OTHERS

Another favorite golf quote of mine is from Ben Hogan, who said, "The most important shot in golf is the next one." To me, this statement is significant. Not only am I getting another shot at rebuilding the life I left behind, but I have the opportunity to do better and help spread the joy of the game to others who may be experiencing a rough time in their lives.

There are many people living right here in Cedar Falls and Waterloo, Iowa, who can benefit from organized adaptive golf events where people with any type of disability can participate and have fun, learn some tips to improve their experience, and meet other people who enjoy the game.

In less than two years, our foundation has been able to raise enough money to purchase four Solo Rider adaptive golf carts and donate them to our four community golf courses. We have begun to expand our reach to the rest of the state, and our vision is to make Iowa a destination for adaptive golf events. We continue to conduct annual adaptive golf clinics and fundraising events to spread our message and grow the number of opportunities for people to come out, enjoy the game, and take their next shot. Everyone needs such a goal, and we want to help them achieve it.

Steve Husome is the director of operations at Clark & Associates Prosthetics and Orthotics and the founder and president of the HusomeStrong Foundation & Adaptive Golf Iowa non-profit organizations. Before his injury, Steve was the 2005 Jones Flight Champion in the Michelob Ultra Golf Tour (Golf Channel Amateur Tour). Since his return to golf competition as an amputee, he has placed in national and Midwest-level amputee tournaments as well as competitions in Iowa, Wisconsin, Missouri, and Nebraska. He is married to his high school sweetheart, and they have two children and two grandchildren.

GOLF GAVE ME MY LIFE BACK

PATTI VALERO

"When people tell me they can't do something, I encourage them to find a way to make it work."

In 2009, I was hit by a drunk driver going the wrong way on the road. I was 43 years old and lost the lower half of my right leg. Before the accident, my main sport was bowling. I was actually working my way up the rankings and was almost able to compete professionally before I was injured. After I lost my leg, it was harder to hold on to the heavy ball while trying to keep my balance.

That is when I turned to golf. I wanted a sport that I felt I could be good at and that I could play with my prosthetic leg. I mainly started playing just so I had something to do while being outside.

FINDING THE COMPETITION

I was working in the fire service at the time, so I was very active and wasn't too concerned with finding a high-endurance sport. I went out and bought thirty dollars-worth of clubs and started playing at a local course. Some older gentlemen at the driving range started coaching me a little bit, and I was hooked immediately. I then started playing more with my husband, who was always a golfer, so he was very good at teaching me all the fundamentals.

I soon moved to Tampa Bay, Florida. Once I knew I had the skills to compete, I started getting involved in different leagues around the area. In every tournament I competed in, I was the only amputee. This actually didn't bother me much; I was proud to show able-bodied people what I was capable of doing as an amputee. Eventually, I decided I wanted to compete against other people with disabilities.

I started talking with people online since I found out most adaptive programs at the time were actually out of state. I eventually connected with someone from the Georgia State Golf Association (GSGA), which has a prominent adaptive golf program. I competed in my first tournament through the GSGA about two years after my accident. My husband and I both competed. He won the able-bodied division, and I won the gross scores for the amputee division.

My first major tournament was at the 2019 Canadian Open. Now, I almost always have something happening with my golf game. I am either practicing with my coach, out playing rounds for fun or even practicing in my backyard. Currently, I am the chairman of a league in Orlando with some PGA pros. It is mainly for disabled military and first responders. They have tournaments every two weeks.

We teach them how to play, and then we take them out and break them into teams so they can play against each other. It sometimes takes a while, but once they get out onto the course, they love it. It lights a fire inside them that they thought was gone, and they are instantly hooked. They listen to me well because I worked with a fire department for many years, and my dad had a military career. We have a staff of eight to ten volunteers, and our players vary from about ten to twenty players. We also have a partnership with our local VA hospital, so they send players over as well.

PARALLELS TO LIFE

I have always played sports, and I have always been very competitive. I went through a string of instructors and finally found one I really liked. She has totally changed my game and has also helped me prepare mentally for every competition. Winning is a lot more than a trophy for me. It is a win for all disabled people and, specifically, all adaptive golfers. When you have those wins under your belt, people become more interested in listening to what you have to say.

When I lost my leg and couldn't work in firefighting, golf was a great thing to try. Golf and firefighting have a lot of parallels. In golf, you have one shot to land on the green, and in the fire service, you have one chance to go in and fight a fire and maybe save lives. In the fire service, you fight and train for disaster, and it is the same in golf. I have the same confidence playing golf that I had on duty with the fire service. Having the confidence to get out on the course is a big part of how I can play as well as I do.

When I hear about someone who needs to have an amputation, I always show them pictures of the incredible tournaments I have been able to participate in and tell them how much I enjoy playing. It is a good re-focus tool for them to understand what they may be able to do rather than concentrate solely on their loss.

I also use my experience to tell people in my league to trust their bodies when they have a hip replacement or something that needs an adaptation. When people tell me they can't do something, I encourage them to find a way to make it work. That is what I did, and it has really paid off. I had to figure out things on my own, and other people must do the same for themselves too.

WHAT AMPUTEES CAN DO

When I first started playing, I didn't want everyone watching me. Now, I love It. I am always finding more people to play with because showing people what you can do builds confidence. That confidence eventually landed me on the Ladies Professional Golf Association (LPGA) Amateur Tour.

I play golf so much because I am afraid to miss that one person who needs to see and understand what amputee golfers can do. I try to golf as much as I can because it means a lot to me. I also understand that this is a world of convenience, and I want to make it easier for as many people as possible to incorporate golf into their life.

Golf gave me my life back. It gave me a purpose. It revealed to me why my accident happened. Golf runs through me as an amputee golfer, and it begs me to go out and share that with people. We live in a body-conscious world, and golf helps me go through life gracefully. It is always a joy to play golf with someone who has never been on the course with an amputee. You can watch their amazement and see their mind shift right in front of your eyes. It's an incredible thing to witness.

Patti Valero hails from Fayetteville, North Carolina but moved a lot as a child for her father's military career. She is the youngest of four children from a very close family. Patti is the mother of three

children and is currently married and residing in Tampa, Florida. She worked part-time at the firehouse and a hospital but currently is an inspirational speaker and, of course, plays a lot of golf.

FINDING THAT COMPETITIVE EDGE

RANDY CLAY

"Golf is a great way to just get out and do something."

I was diagnosed with bone cancer in 2004, when I was 39 years old. After chemotherapy and other medical interventions, the end result was the loss of my right leg at the knee. Before this all happened, I was always a very competitive person. I played golf, basketball, and travel softball for a while. When I lost my leg, I was pretty worried that I would not be able to find that competitive edge ever again.

RETURN TO GOLF

A year later, when I was done with all my treatment and officially cancer free, I felt a strong urge to get out and play golf again. I basically picked up right where I left off. It was a little hard to keep my balance for a while but other than that, I had no problem swinging a club. After getting out and practicing a few times, I had no issues. I also figured out that there were other prosthetics out there that would work better for golf. Now, I have a regular walking prosthetic and another one that I use specifically when I'm out on the course. The golfing prosthetic allows for better balance and makes it easier for me to turn through my swing.

I started listening to whatever lessons or advice I could get from course professionals, coaches, and even my friends. I tried to stay open-minded when it came to learning how to play golf as an amputee. In the long run, I think this really paid off.

I started with an adaptive golf competition at The Phoenix Cup in Florida in 2018, an international event. I had only played in one adaptive golf tournament before that. The Phoenix Cup was amazing. I couldn't believe how well everyone with all different disabilities played the game. I had no problem competing. I always have a lot of confidence in myself, so competing at such a big international tournament for the first time was no issue. If I want to do something, then I just go do it.

I have been involved heavily in golf ever since. Every time one of my friends in the world of adaptive golf needs a person to play, I am there on the course with no questions asked. I have made many great friends through adaptive golf. I have loved hearing so many different amazing stories, and of course, to see adaptive golf grow so much as it has over the last couple of years.

IN SERVICE TO GOLF

I try to help as many people as I can with adaptive golf. I have a lot of other skills, too, including working with my hands as a mechanic. The Southwest Amputee Golf Association enlisted my help when they needed a SoloRider golf cart. I was able to locate one that needed a lot of maintenance, and then I worked on it and drove it out to them in Texas. It was rewarding to know that the SoloRider was going to help introduce people to adaptive golf. I am also working on getting another cart for a friend of mine who recently lost both of his legs. It would be rewarding to introduce him to adaptive golf as well.

In addition to golfing, I do a lot of deer hunting and fishing. My amputation doesn't affect these activities much, except I can't stalk deer well anymore. I spend most of my time stationary in a blind. If I have my head up looking around for deer, I am more likely to trip on my prosthetic and fall.

In order to challenge someone to get into adaptive golf, I would tell them golf is a great way to just get out and do something. You don't have to play well; you should just get out and enjoy it, whether you are a true beginner or someone who used to play. You can get exercise, enjoy the outdoors, and meet new people all at the same time. It is really mind over matter; it's all in the attitude.

A WINNING ATTITUDE

To me, golf is always competitive because I have always been a competitive person. My attitude is the same with every round. Even in my men's league, I play like my life depends on it. I want to earn the absolute best possible score I can, every time. Even when I play cards with my wife, I have that mindset. It's just the way I am.

Currently, golf is something I get to do two or three times a week. It is important for my physical and mental health, and I love to go out, meet new people, and see new places. It's definitely one of my most favorite parts of the game. As for my achievements, my proudest moment is still being a member of the 2018 Phoenix Cup USA Team. I'm glad to know that even as an amputee, I have not lost my competitive edge. You don't have to lose yours, either!

Randy Clay lives in southwest Florida, near Fort Myers. He works at a golf course as a member of the grounds crew and regularly mows the fairways. He has been married to his wonderful wife for twenty years and has three grown children.

GOLF IS EVERYTHING

STEVE SHIPULESKI

"It is always valuable to try something new and outside of your comfort zone."

I was born several weeks premature with nerve damage to my left hand. My left leg is also shorter than my right one, but that has never stopped me from being active. I grew up working on a farm in Connecticut and quickly learned to adapt my abilities to do what needed to be done. I have always loved being active.

I never actually thought about golf until I was 26 years old. After attending an outing with my then-girlfriend, I went out and spent the day on the practice range while she played in the event. It was 1995 then, and I played my first full round of eighteen holes just a year later.

Immediately, I realized I was hooked.

CALL OF THE COURSE

It started as recreation, but it has grown into a super-passion for competing. My current wife talked me into playing in the Florida Adaptive Open six years ago, and I have won it four times since.

Like all adaptive golfers, I have overcome a lot. While I haven't sustained a life-changing injury like some, my passion for golf is unmatched. I really hope that people see my enthusiasm for the game and that it will convince other people with similar disabilities to get involved in adaptive golf. The best way to approach the sport is to be enthusiastic about playing. It doesn't even matter if you care about how you play; instead, just enjoy the fact that you're playing!

I currently live near West Palm Beach, Florida, but I travel all over the country, competing in adaptive tournaments wherever I can find them. I believe I was one of the farthest-traveled players in the field of 61 players at this year's Midwest Amputee Golf Association All Disability Open in Tinley Park, Illinois. Competing is in my blood, and I just love it. I particularly love the tournaments where I can compete in match play.

Like me, my wife loves to golf as well. The two of us get out and play at least once a week. I love watching her play, and she loves watching me play. Both of us give each other tips on how to improve on different areas of our game, and we love getting together with friends to play too. I feel very lucky that golf plays such a prominent role in my marriage. I also love that I have the opportunity to show able-bodied golfers what people with disabilities like me are capable of doing on the course. At a 7 handicap, I actually play a lot better than most of my able-bodied friends.

I have always tried to get other people with disabilities involved in golf. I think the best way to do that is to show off your enthusiasm for the game. When other disabled people see how much I love golf, I think they might feel inclined to try it as well. Since I have received so much from golf, I know it can help other people too, so I really want to get as many other people involved as possible. I think using my passion for golf is the best way to show people like me that golf can open up a whole new world of opportunities to compete, meet other adaptive golfers, and just to be outside in nature.

A PERFECT FIT

I have never been that athletic, so I was very happy to find a sport that I could play without being in especially good shape. Also, I became an accomplished golfer quite quickly, thanks to a lot of coaching and hard work. It made me so happy to find a sport that I was able to play as someone with a physical disability. When I was teaching myself how to play golf, I never even actually thought about my disability. I just tried to figure out how to make it work, which I eventually did.

Even after playing for so many years, golf is still everything to me. I live and breathe golf. I think about it constantly. It means that much to me, and it will always mean that much to me. I have a side-arm swing form, which I realize is a little unorthodox. But, during my learning process, I found that it's the form that works best for me. Once I found my swing, working on chipping and putting came pretty easily to me.

I am someone who came to this game by chance, but I would challenge other disabled athletes to make an effort to get out and play because it truly does a lot of good for the soul. Since I knew nothing about golf before my girlfriend convinced me to go hit a few balls, I truly believe it is always valuable to try something new and outside of your comfort zone. You never know where it might take you.

In my case, adaptive golf took me all over the country for tournaments. It brought me a lot of new friends, and it opened up a world of possibilities for me. If you take that same leap, it might just be the best decision you have ever made.

Steve Shipuleski currently works as a director at an insulation company. Besides that, everything he does revolves around the game of golf. He moved from Connecticut to Florida to play twelve months out of the year, and he now plays four to five times a week. He also builds clubs in his garage and tries them out on the practice range.

LIVING UP TO THE CHALLENGE

STEVEN FORD

"It's just as satisfying to hit a beautiful shot in front of a crowd as it is by yourself."

I was in a motorcycle accident 11 years ago, at the age of 20. I landed on my right arm as I slid across the pavement. As a result, I suffered severe nerve damage and have no use of my right arm at all.

I have been playing golf my whole life. I was a tournament player as a young child. I have only played one-arm golf for about six years. Truthfully, I didn't think about returning to golf after my accident. One day I just thought I could get out and chip around and do some light-swing stuff around my yard. Eventually, I figured it out. Hey, I can do this, I thought to myself. That's when I found the North American One-Armed Golfer Association. (NAOAGA).

ACTIVE IN ADAPTIVE

I swing backhand since my left arm is the only one that

works. This is just what came naturally to me since I was a right-handed golfer for years. Turning my body, playing with left-handed clubs, and playing forehanded with my left hand never even crossed my mind.

I have been a competitor and ambassador with NAOAGA for four years, and I was also elected to the board of directors. I have always enjoyed the community, and it is nice to play with people who have the same disability as me, so I naturally gravitated to the organization. They run world-class events with the U.S. Adaptive Golf Alliance. The first tournament I played in was in Michigan at Tree Tops Resort, and it was awesome. You come for the golf and compete, but you end up sticking around for the people. You look forward to seeing your friends at each event even more than actually playing golf.

I have played in the Fightmaster Cup in 2018, the one-armed version of the Ryder Cup in Europe. The Fightmaster Cup was against the European Society of One-Armed Golfers. We played in Kent, England, right on the White Cliffs of Dover. The people were amazing and very welcoming, but the conditions were brutal. It rained, with high winds, but that made the experience even more unique. Each day after the match was over, both teams were very friendly towards one other, even though we were all fighting pretty hard for the win.

I also helped with the Georgia State Golf Association (GSGA) clinics quite regularly, along with Dave Windsor, one of the biggest advocates for adaptive golf instruction. He is one of the guys that kicked it off. I became a certified coach through

Dave. In adaptive golf, it is a natural progression to become good at golf and then pass on that knowledge to other people. It is not unlike my work as an auto mechanic. If you find somebody with a broken-down car and you have the skill to help them fix it, you naturally feel inclined to help them. Likewise, it is also very valued and appreciated to have one-armed golfers coached by other one-armed golfers.

HARD WORK PAYS

In the last four years, I have put a lot of time and effort into improving my game. I have had some elbow problems, so I am also starting to change up my swing to forehand, and I am making good progress. It has been a long, tough road, filled with a lot of hard work, but it has really paid off for me. This is something I always try to show one-armed golfers who are new to the game. Hard work always pays off.

When you challenge someone to get into golf, how they'll do actually depends on where they are in their game and their attitude. Often, it is all about motivation and convincing them that they can do more than they think they can. They must know that golfing will get them out of the house and help them meet or spend time with friends. Golfing is something that everyone can do, regardless of disability or ability.

For people just getting started in adaptive golf, it is important to stress that the game can be as competitive as they want it to be, and if they like competition, there will be plenty of opportunities. The competition was actually what hooked me, but for other people, it is the camaraderie of being with golfers who have a similar disability. With adaptive golf, you can enjoy both competition and camaraderie at the same time. You don't have to choose.

It is hard to explain how much golf means to me because I have played for as long as I can remember. I love the fact that it is outdoors in a natural setting and that it is brutally competitive. I also love how I can enjoy it just by myself. Some of the best shots I have hit have not been seen by anybody, and they don't need to be seen by anybody. I usually don't even tell anyone. It's just as satisfying to hit a beautiful shot in front of a crowd as it is all by yourself. That is what keeps me coming back. It gives me a productive, healthy focal point and something to keep foremost in my mind. People find their "thing," and mine has always been golf. And I think it always will be.

Steven Ford was born and raised in Rome, Georgia, where he currently resides. He is the general manager of his dad's auto body shop, having been raised in the business. At first, only having use of one arm was difficult, but just as in golf, Steven rose to the challenge. He began with administration but can now perform any maintenance needed on his customers' vehicles.

IMPROVE EVERY DAY

TRACY RAMIN

"It is good to challenge yourself and to help challenge others."

When I was 26 years old, I was working in construction. I was driving down a highway when a ladder fell off the back of my truck. I pulled over and got out to move the ladder out of the middle of the road. Another truck was speeding at about 80 miles per hour in a 55 miles per hour speed zone, so he obviously could not stop in time before hitting me. I was thrown more than 100 yards from the spot where I was hit. I broke both my legs and dislocated my right shoulder so severely that my mobility is still significantly limited. I lost all but two quarts of blood, and I was given a ten percent chance to survive the accident. I survived, but I ended up losing my left leg.

COMPELLED TO COMPETE

Before that, I was a pretty solid golfer. I played all the time and often shot in the low 80s. After my injury, I immediately started thinking of how I was going to play golf again. My prosthetist at the time introduced me to the Michigan Amputee Golf Association. I spent some time learning about what they did and how they helped out people like me. It took about a year to approach the organization. They gave me a lot of hope. I could not wait to get back out onto the golf course.

I knew golf was going to be especially challenging as an amputee, but I wanted to get back into it anyway. After I started playing with a prosthetic left leg, I realized golf was something I could still do at a high level. Eventually, I started competing in adaptive golf tournaments in places like Chicago and Atlanta. I started playing in the Michigan Amputee Golf Association's (MAGA) Amputee Tournament in 2007. Immediately, I was in awe of the number of people with amputations like me who were there to compete in golf. I've always been a solid golfer, but right away, I realized that I was getting outplayed by a lot of other amputees. It was then that I adopted a whole new attitude and work ethic.

I started working on my game almost every day. I analyzed every area, every stroke. I started improving, but it still took me four years until I won MAGA's tournament in 2010. I have won it four times since then, along with a few other tournaments around the country.

One of my favorite parts of being involved in adaptive golf is all the traveling I get to do and all the incredible people I get to meet. At first, it was just a way for me to learn how to play with my own prosthetic, but it eventually turned into a way of life. That way of life included involvement with organizations like Freedom Golf Association (FGA). It was here that I met Jonathan Snyder, one of the first people I had the opportunity to observe as an adaptive golf instructor. It didn't take long before I noticed how much good golf could do for younger people with disabilities. Going around and seeing the smiling faces of kids at clinics and camps made me realize how much golf really does for young people with disabilities.

From there, I was able to actually become part of growing the game. I participated in more clinics and even outings, where I witnessed how much fun other disabled people of all ages were having out on the golf course.

I feel very fortunate to have had a front-row seat to watch some incredible adaptive golfers. Without them, this game would not be where it is today. We wouldn't have tournaments all over the country, giving people the opportunity to show off how much they've learned and really put it to the test while going up against other adaptive golfers.

UP TO THE CHALLENGE

Golf is a challenge, but I truly think it is good to challenge yourself and to help challenge others. If someone just had a similar accident like the one I had when I was 26 and they were apprehensive about getting into golf, I would challenge them to just pick up a club and get out and play. I made that decision a long time ago, and it was the best decision I ever made. Since then, I have learned that the adaptive golf community is actually just one big family.

If someone is struggling to get out and be active, I wouldn't want them to be struggling to make friends either. Getting involved in adaptive golf is the perfect way to do both. I have met so many friends through golf that I know will be with me throughout my life. It is also very nice to know people who have survived the same hardships that I have. I never would have met such people if it weren't for golf. It just demonstrates how tough and strong-willed adaptive golfers are. They all overcame something terrible to prove to people that they are still capable of playing this great game. And they do it so very well!

Tracy Ramin was born and raised in Michigan and currently lives in a town called Montrose with his girlfriend, Tonia. He has a

21-year-old son and a 25-year-old daughter who recently gave birth to his first granddaughter. Tracy works as a teaching professional at two different golf clubs: Briar Ridge Golf Club and Beachwood Greens. Tracy also owns several massage chairs in malls across four different states and tries to play golf almost every day. Golf is, and always will be, a huge part of his life.

SHOOTING TO THE TOP

KEVIN HOLLAND

"Never quit."

When people ask me to tell them the story of how I became disabled, I tell them I was simply born with cerebral palsy, with no brain tissue on my left side. Doctors did not expect me to ever walk, talk, sit, or stand, let alone golf. To this day, I have limited mobility in my right arm. And although I do have some peripheral vision on my right side, I cannot turn my head to see you.

Yet, I'm currently making my way to number one as a top-rank, one-arm golfer through the North American One Arm Golfers Association (NAOAGA) and the World Ranking for Golfers with Disabilities. I am considered an "assisted player" because when I address the golf ball, I physically touch my right arm onto the club and then take it away. Golf is more than a sport to me; it's a life mission to become the best golfer I can be.

FROM CASUAL TO COMPETITOR

My dad introduced me to golf when I was 10 years old. He would play for business and would often take me with him. I took lessons and played and loved the game but wasn't very competitive about it until my basketball coach in high school began to take an interest in me. He also happened to be the school golf coach, and he convinced me to try out for the golf team in my senior year and gave me some good coaching on my game.

One day in 2017, I was out on the course when I ran into my friend Xander Dobriff. He was recuperating from a car accident, and although nothing was unusual about his appearance, the accident left him unable to feel the golf club in one of his hands. That's how I found out about the North American One Arm Golf Association and began getting involved.

INTRO TO ADAPTIVE

At first, Xander and I played "standard" events together at a U.S. Amateur tour (USAM), and we were the only two one-armed golfers in the field. Then we played a NAOAGA tournament at the Treetop Resort in Gaylord, Michigan, in 2016. At the time, I had a 35 handicap. It was exhausting but exciting to play 10 days of golf and stay up late every night meeting new people. I came home and slept for three days.

The rest is history. The first year, I worked with my coach to develop my swing and get better at the game. I kept perfecting my craft and competing as much as I could. Now I'm going out and playing at high-level tournaments, meeting the right people in the right organizations, and making true friends.

Over the past three years, I've climbed from a ranking of 220th in my division worldwide to 129th. Two years ago, I might be able to drive 250 yards, but it was 200 yards straight with a 50-yard slice. Now, I am capable of hitting the ball 280 yards down the middle. This year, I played the tournament at Treetop again, this time with a 9.8 handicap. I felt like I had come full circle!

ALL IN THE ATTITUDE

There's a slogan in the NAOAGA: "never quit." That's the secret to my success. I've worked harder to improve my golfing than I have at anything in my life. When I found out there was a world ranking for disabled golfers, I set my goal to someday be number one.

As I moved into a lower handicap within the NAOAGA and world rank for disability, I knew that the competition would increase, so I had to be ready. My coach and I spent November of 2019 trying different clubs and fitting my grip down from a 74-gram shaft to a 55-gram shaft, which dramatically increased my club speed. I was also working out three times a week and practicing at GolfTech to improve my swing.

If I had a rough tournament, I would go back to the drawing board, work with my coach, and pick his brain and ask questions, rather than just continuing on to the next tournament.

Currently, golf is a second job for me. I'm not getting paid yet for it yet, but I'm trying to get sponsors and ambassador deals. In the meantime, I'm happy to inspire two-armed golfers whenever I can, including out on the golf course where I work, The Orchards in Washington, Michigan. I am a member of the grounds crew, setting up the reservations and doing whatever needs to be done.

People tell me I'm an inspiration and even ask to film me out on the golf course. I've been at courses where instructors have brought students over to watch my technique. I've even heard them say to some of their struggling students, "Do you really want to give up? Look at what that guy can do with one arm!"

SET TO INSPIRE

My success in golf has not only changed my life but changed me. I used to be kind of quiet and shy, a laid-back guy. Now, I don't hesitate to speak up, lead by example, and motivate those around me. It's taken a while for me to feel comfortable talking to people, but being successful at golf has brought me out of my shell.

One time I was working when a father and his son came into the clubhouse. I noticed the son's gait and that he was a one-armed golfer, practicing for the Special Olympics.

"Were you born with cerebral palsy?" I asked him. The boy nodded his head. "Me too," I told him.

I spoke with the boy and his father for some time, and I

gave him my number and said I hoped we could get together and go golfing one day. Since then, I have become friends with Lucas and his family, have mentored his game, and opened many doors for him. I've helped him understand that there's a future in golf for him and an organization that can help him learn a game he can grow into.

As for me, my golf dream is to drop another seven shots from my game and, ultimately, to turn pro. I'm very proud to be a world-ranked golfer, and I'm shooting to be among the best of the best, scoring in the 70's.

Everyone in this book is a huge inspiration and exemplary ambassadors to the game of golf, including my friend Johnathan Snyder. We are all different in our own way, and we all have different swings. But we're all included, and that's what the game is all about!

Kevin Holland is a world-ranked golfer and can regularly be seen on the courses in tournament play for the Michigan Amputee Golfers Association, the North American One Arm Golfers Association, and the National Amputee Golfers Association.

THE OVERCOMER

JONATHAN SNYDER

"In golf and in life, there is a lesson in staying positive. You can achieve so much more!"

I was born in Charlotte, North Carolina and grew up as quite the athlete. I excelled in many sports, but especially basketball. I played Amateur Athletic Union (AAU) basketball all through high school. However, I was different than the rest of the guys on the team. I was born with a below the elbow limb deficiency, an undeveloped left hand without fingers.

I was teased about it when I was a child and teenager, but that didn't stop me from working hard at adapting to my unique challenges. My parents brought me up in a faith-filled environment, focusing on Jesus. They treated me as if I could do everything I set my mind to do, which I believe contributes to my success. I just allowed my mind and athleticism to shine and became an "overcomer" of everything that was placed in front of me.

FAMILY RESPONSIBILITY

When I was 18 years old and just about to head off to college, my father was involved in an accident at work that severed four of his fingers on his left hand. I had a change of heart, and a change of plans about college. Instead, I stayed home to help him run his contracting company, Design II, for 4 years until my father was back running it full time. We were recognized as one of the top contractors in the area, so I did my best to keep the family business running successfully and managed to do so too.

My Father's accident while scary brought us closer together. Because of my personal experience, I was able to teach my dad how to do things without having fingers on his left hand. I showed him the best way to tie a shoelace and button up his shirt buttons. I even taught him how to swing a golf club. Sports brought us closer together as I encouraged him not to let his new challenge get in his way of achievement, as he had always encouraged me to overcome all obstacles. It's about adapting to each situation the life presents.

At the time I was 22 years old, I started playing golf regularly. Very quickly, it became my passion, and positive therapy for me. I started working on the cart staff at the Red Bridge Golf Club in Locust, North Carolina as a volunteer. I eventually worked my way up the ranks from assistant golf professional, to event coordinator, to head golf professional, eventually to general manager of entire golf club. Red Bridge Golf Club gave me the opportunity to excel not only in the game of golf, but in the golf industry itself.

People ask me the secret to my success, and I say that "To have a positive outcome in golf, we have to have a great attitude". I try to always keep a positive attitude and try not to look at the negative things. It also doesn't take a pro to realize that I'm not just talking about golf. There's a life lesson in staying positive. You can achieve so much more!

COMPETITIVE EDGE

The year 2017 was pivotal for me. I was invited to compete in the Para-Long Drive National Championships at Legends Resort by Alan Gentry, the founder of the North American One-Armed Golf Association. I finished second in my division, and it was at this event that I was welcomed into the adaptive golf community by gentlemen like Tracy Ramin and Steven Ford, who have since become some of my closest friends. The adaptive golf community is so welcoming, and I'm so grateful for their inclusion. In 2017, I also won the Club Championship at Red Bridge, and was selected to be on United States Para- Golf Team to conduct exhibitions.

In 2018, I accepted the position of adaptive golf director at Freedom Golf Association (FGA) just outside of Chicago. It was then that I became trained in Adaptive Golf Instruction by my mentor David Windsor PGA. He is the Adaptive Golf Director for the GSGA (Georgia State Golf Association) The Freedom Golf Association brings joy and a sense of freedom to individuals with special needs and wounded veterans through their inclusion in the game of golf.

Instructing and giving Adaptive golf lessons is now my passion in life. As FGA's director of golf operations, and I created a model that provides a record number of adaptive golf lessons every year. We conducted 6,755 adaptive golf lessons in 2018, 9,499 in 2019, and 3,775 in 2020, putting FGA on the forefront of adaptive golf lessons in the United States, and a leading organization within the 38 member organizations within the United States Adaptive Golf Alliance.

I also compete regularly in adaptive golf tournaments throughout the country, encouraging others to begin to compete. In 2018, I was selected to be the captain of the Phoenix Cup team for team USA and that same year I was selected to be on the Fightmaster Cup team through the North American One Arm Golf Association, a one-arm version of the Ryder Ciup that took place at Walmer-Kingsdown Golf Club in Dover, England. In 2018, I was also asked to become the Vice president of the Midwestern Amputee Golf Association, alongside President Bradley Schubert.

This year (2020), I was selected Vice captain of the Cairns Cup team, a pan-disability Ryder Cup style event that will take place at Celtic Manor in the United Kingdom. Together with Tracy Ramin (Captain) and John Bell (Vice captain), we plan to represent the United States of America with pride and joy providing to upmost respect for our opponents from Team Europe.

Currently, I reside just outside of Chicago with my fiancé,

Michala Mika, and my daughter Lillian. Michala is no stranger to golf, playing college golf & is now the director for Kids Golf Foundation of Illinois and helps thousands of children enjoy the game of golf each year. Most events she caddies for me, and I attribute much of my recent success on the course to Michala's guidance and support.

I'm grateful to have found adaptive golf so I can share my passion & bring more individuals to enjoy the benefits of the game. It is a positive way, and my favorite way, to enjoy life each and every day.

Jonathan Snyder competes in numerous tournaments throughout the United States and could use your help with sponsorships. These sponsorships can help Jonathan compete and continue his adaptive advocacy work across the country. Jonathan Snyder currently serves as the director of golf operations at United States Adaptive Golf Alliance and resides with his fiancé, Michala Mika, and his daughter in the Chicago area.

GOLF IS MEANT FOR ANYBODY

BRANDON CANESI

When my mom was pregnant with me, she was given medication to induce her period. This happened because she was given the results of someone else's test that showed she was not pregnant. That medication killed the twin fetus she was carrying with me, and caused me to be born without hands. This medication had been known at the time to cause these kind of terrible side effects. Unfortunately, my mom never knew any of that. As a kid, I never saw myself has that different from anyone else. Obviously, I knew I had to adapt but I always felt just as normal.

I was always involved in a number of sports, basketball, baseball, soccer, and of course golf. The first time I touched a club was when I was visiting my Grandfather down in Florida. I began playing with the club tucked under my arm when I was 6 years old. I immediately fell in love with the sport. I grew out of being able to do that, so I stopped playing until I was about 16.

I adapted to that by making my own clubs. We used steel shafts, and molded them together so the clubs were longer. We also put in big putter grips that allow me to hold it under my arm. Now, every time I am out on the golf course, I feel like I was born to play golf. This sport has always been in my family, so being able to play has been a blessing to me because it has brought me closer to them. It also makes me feel close to my deceased Grandfather, who was really the one that got me into playing.

In 2016, I started a foundation called "Hole High." I took videos of myself golfing, and shared them all over social media. I also hosted a tournament in my hometown, with about 80 of my friends and family. This tournament raised $15,000. Most of that money I donated back to Shriners Hospital for Children, where I spent a lot of time as a kid. Giving back is always something that I really love doing now.

When I was 25, I went to the Golf Academy of America in Myrtle Beach, South Carolina. 2 months into the Academy, I made a hole-in-one that I actually caught on video during one of our practice rounds. It went viral, about 3 million views in 1 week, and I got a lot of encouragement to keep playing from people all over the world. From there, I started getting a lot of media attention, and even sponsorships from big golf companies like TaylorMade. The Golf Academy unfortunately lost their funding and closed down before I had a chance to graduate.

When you wake up each morning without hands, you tend to repeatedly ask yourself "Why." Golf made me feel like that question was being answered. Golf is the main reason I moved to the Miami Area when I was hired as an Assistant

Pro at Trump National Doral. I moved around there, and I was eventually promoted to Outside Operations Manager. I work really hard to show people how I can play golf because I think it is really important to showcase what people with disabilities are really capable of. Even though the content I share is just of me, it really helps disabled people and adaptive golf as a whole. All of the content I have put out has had a pretty large following, and everybody is usually very positive and encouraging. That is really what fuels my fair to keep playing.

I first competed in the USDGA Open in Orlando in 2018. I played with Tracy Ramin, one of the biggest names in Adaptive Golf. He was blown away with my ability, and he was the one that really convinced me to get more involved. I was immediately fixated on how amazing all those other golfers were as players with all different disabilities. I realized that must be how people feel when they see me play, it was really cool.

I eventually went with Tracy and the US Adaptive Golf team to Las Vegas to give a clinic to Shriners ambassadors. We got to hit balls with guys like Rickie Fowler and Bubba Watson too, which was really cool. The energy I got from these kids with all different disabilities was unbelievable. This was the best experience I have had in golf. My heart was so full watching these kids pick up a club for the first time and immediately become hooked.

I do get messages all the time from people that are interested in finding clubs like mine so they can learn to play with no hands. I always tell them to start by finding a way that works for you. Golf starts with determination and focus, once you find that, you can learn this incredibly difficult game. Golf tests every characteristic of yourself, and it is all about asking yourself "how hard are you willing to work at it."

Golf taught me that hard work mentality. Before getting into the Golf Academy, I was a community college student making really poor grades, and my mind was never into it. That changed at the Academy. I knew I was going to be 100% invested in acing every test, completing every homework assignment, and of course playing the best golf possible. Golf is meant to be played by anybody, with anybody. I don't care how good you are, I don't care what your ability is, you get out on the course and you play. That is all that matters.

I was born and raised in New Jersey, in 2019 I moved down to Miami. I live with 2 guys I went to the Academy with, and we all work together at Trump National. We live right by the resort, so it is a great place to work. I get to play quite a bit there for free, and there are 4 courses on the property so I usually don't have much trouble finding times to play.

Made in the USA
Columbia, SC
26 August 2021

43837056R00078